中国と日本のデザイン要素

中國及日本設計要素

Elements of Chinese and Japanese Design

Elementi di design cinese e giapponese
Elementos de design chineses e japoneses
Eléments du design chinois et japonais
Elementos de diseño chinos y japoneses
Designmotive aus China und Japan

中国と日本のデザイン要素

中國及日本設計要素

Elements of Chinese and Japanese Design

Elementi di design cinese e giapponese
Elementos de design chineses e japoneses
Eléments du design chinois et japonais
Elementos de diseño chinos y japoneses
Designmotive aus China und Japan

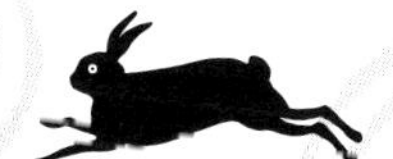

The Pepin Press
Amsterdam and Singapore

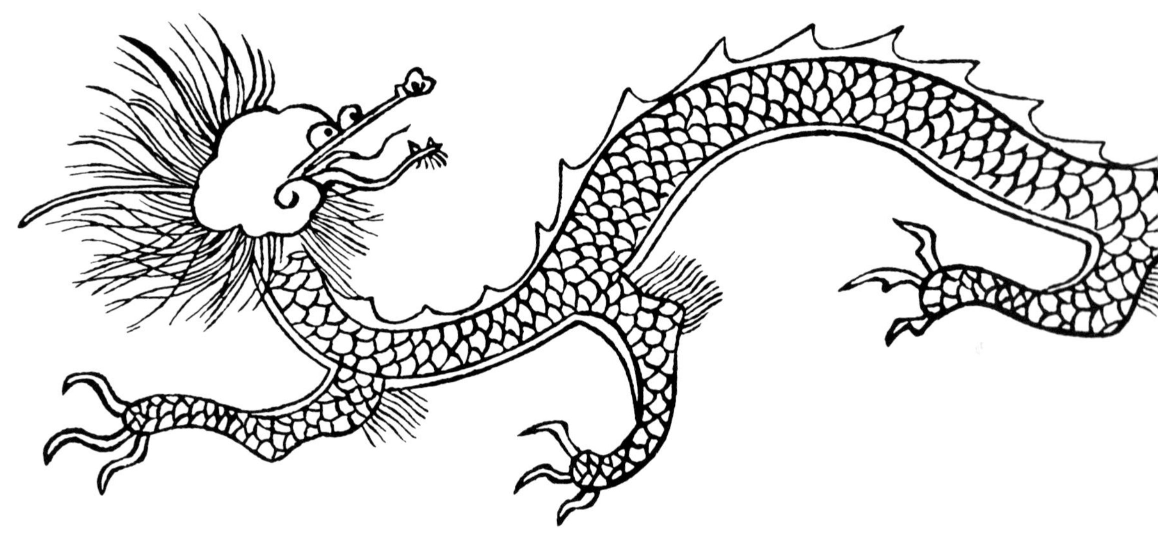

The Pepin Press / Agile Rabbit Editions
P.O. Box 10349
1001 EH Amsterdam, The Netherlands

Tel +31 20 4202021
Fax +31 20 4201152
mail@pepinpress.com
www.pepinpress.com

ISBN 90 5768 042 4

Concept & series editor: Pepin van Roojen
Cover design and layout for this volume: Dorine van den Beukel

10 9 8 7 6 5 4 3 2 1
2007 06 05 04 03 02

Manufactured in Singapore

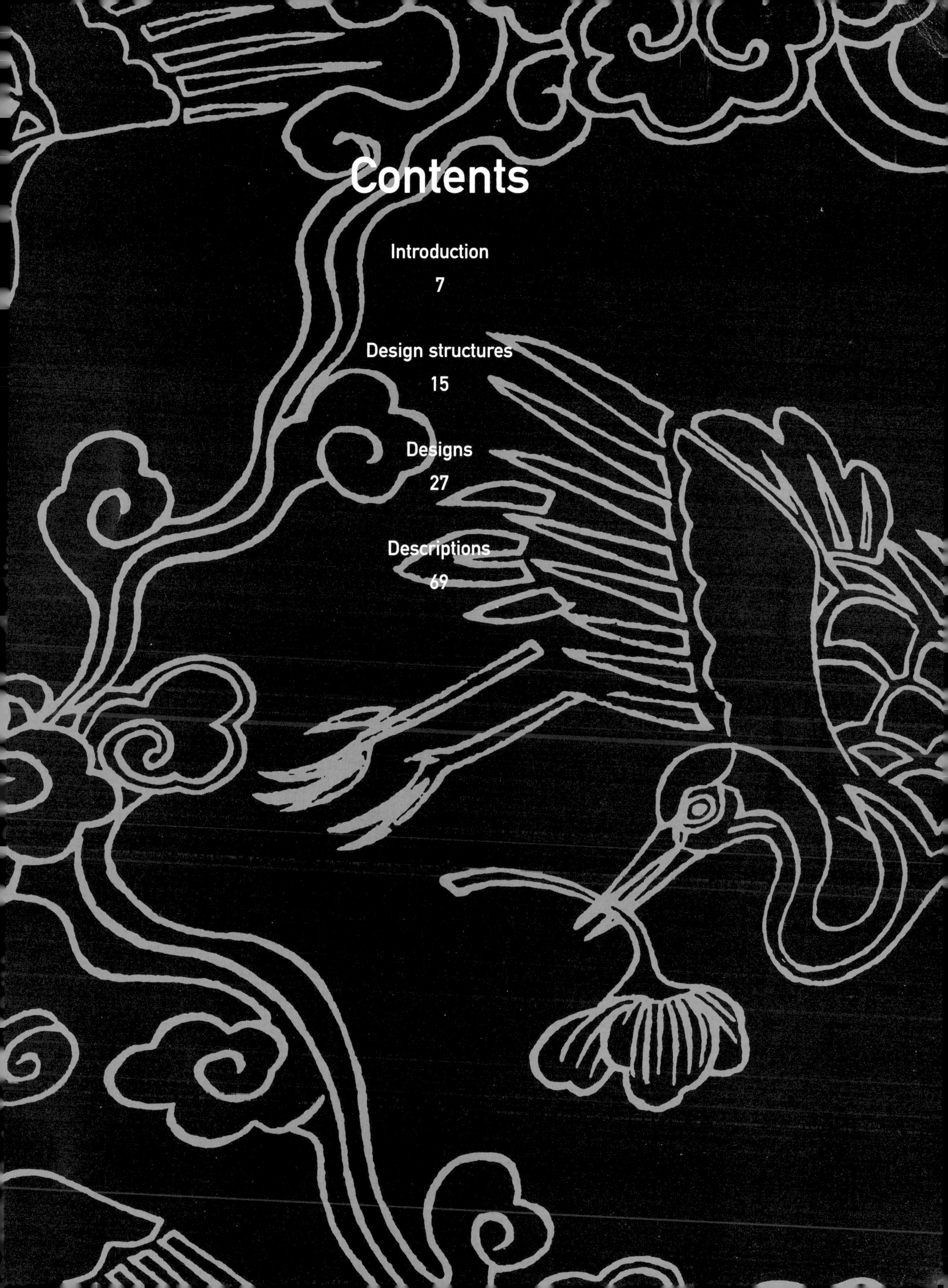

Contents

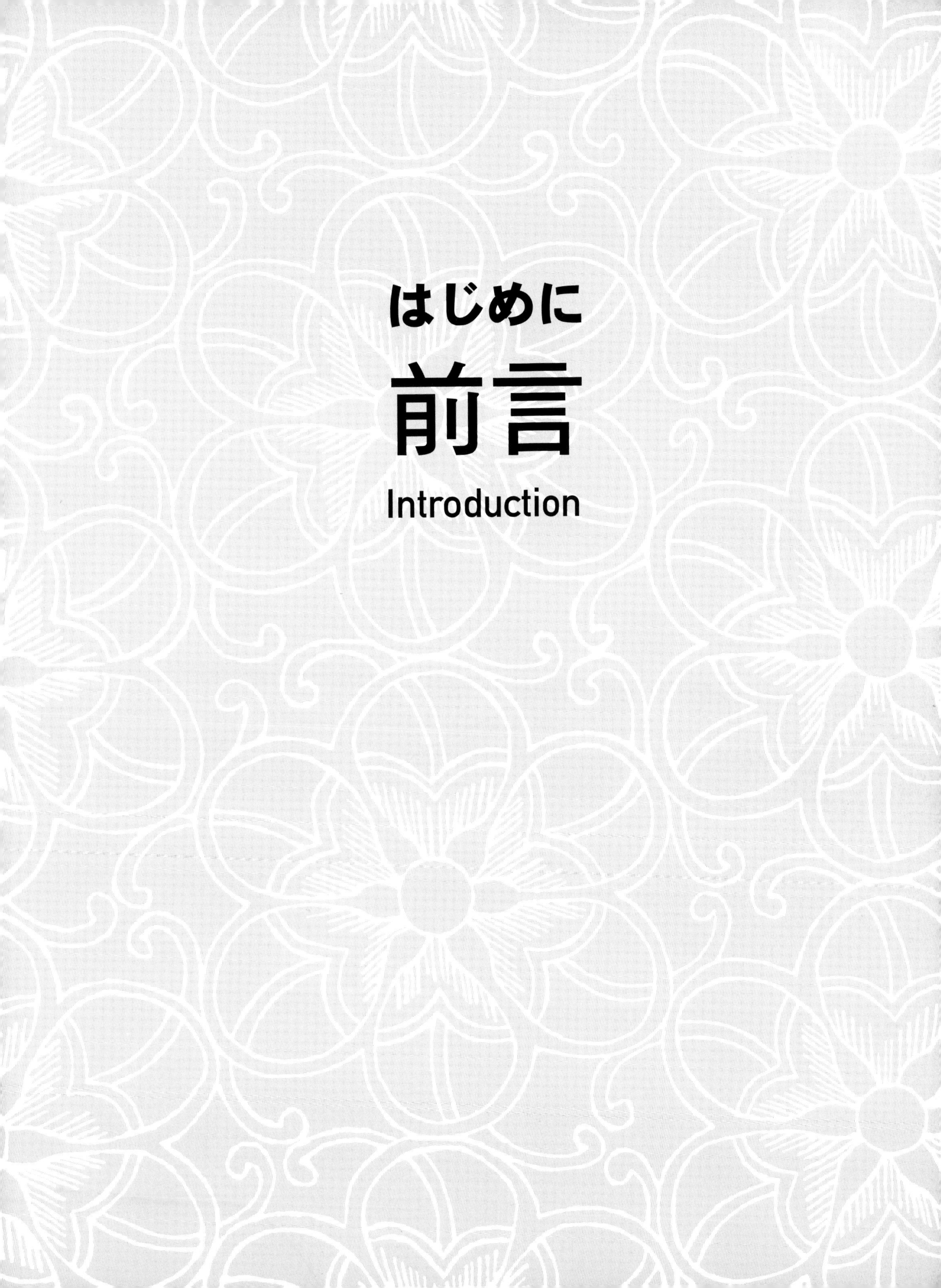

はじめに

前言

Introduction

Elements of Chinese and Japanese Design

China and Japan have ornamental traditions that are among the foremost in the world. Furthermore, the two countries have interchanged elements from their decorative styles, resulting in a partially overlapping visual language.

The collection of designs and patterns presented in this book originates from the 19th century. However, many of the patterns themselves are actually from ancient times, although some appear to be designed in more recent centuries. The designs were collected from a great many sources. In fact, almost all forms of decorative art from China and Japan seem to have been examined to accumulate this profusion of ornamental magnificence. So we can find images derived from various types of textile, embroidery, porcelain, gold, silver, copper and bronze work, but also lacquer work and wall paper.

Some of the designs are clearly regional, originating from a certain area or even city, e.g. Enshu (Totomi) or Kyoto, Kobe or Musashi. From other designs it can be said they are typically Chinese or typically Japanese because of their style and motifs. But in many cases, designs are generic for China and Japan, so these cannot be attributed to any specific place or time.

The motifs used vary from abstract and geometric forms to more realistic images such as playing children or typically Chinese and Japanese objects such as gongs or lanterns. Flowers are a distinct inspiration in Chinese and Japanese design, both in stylised form as in the shape of exact representations. Notably chrysanthemums, bamboo flowers, water-lilies, irises, and peonies occur frequently. Other compositions may be inspired by plants, such as wisteria and ivy, trees (oak, pine), and fruits and vegetables: water-chestnuts, pomegranates, plums, cherries, aubergines, and cucumbers.

Animals appearing in the designs range from small to large: insects, butterflies and fish, elephants and lions, often depicted with balls, flying bats, turtles, rabbits, and many birds: peacocks, swallows, parrots, cranes, sparrows and ducks. In addition to these 'real' animals, mythological animals such the dragon, the kirin, the phoenix and the sai are depicted.

And nature does not stop here as a form of inspiration: rivers, mountains, rain, snow, thunder, clouds, waves – all can be traced as the source of specific designs.

Last but not least, mention should be made of religion and mythology as origins of Chinese and Japanese design. Examples of this are the many mythological beasts, flying figures and symbols appearing throughout this book. An example of the latter is the swastika, a Chinese emblem of happiness, longevity and health.

English

This book contains images for use as a graphic resource, or inspiration. All the illustrations are stored in high-resolution format on the enclosed free CD-ROM (Mac and Windows) and are ready to use for professional quality printed media and web page design. The pictures can also be used to produce postcards, either on paper or digitally, or to decorate your letters, flyers, etc. They can be imported directly from the CD into most design, image-manipulation, illustration, word-processing and e-mail programs; no installation is required. Some programs will allow you to access the images directly; in others, you will first have to create a document, and then import the images. Please consult your software manual for instructions.
The names of the files on the CD-ROM correspond with the page numbers in this book. For pages with more than one image, the order is from left to right and from top to bottom. This is indicated with a number following the page number, or with the following letter codes: T = top, B = bottom, C = centre, L = left, and R = right.
The CD-ROM comes free with this book, but is not for sale separately. The publishers do not accept any responsibility should the CD not be compatible with your system.
For non-professional applications, single images can be used free of charge. The images cannot be used for any type of commercial or otherwise professional application – including all types of printed or digital publications – without prior permission from The Pepin Press/Agile Rabbit Editions.

For inquiries about permissions and fees:
mail@pepinpress.com
Fax +31 20 4201152

Deutsch

Dieses Buch enthält Bilder, die als Ausgangsmaterial für graphische Zwecke oder als Anregung genutzt werden können. Alle Abbildungen sind in hoher Auflösung auf der beiliegenden Gratis-CD-ROM (für Mac und Windows) gespeichert und lassen sich direkt zum Drucken in professioneller Qualität oder zur Gestaltung von Websites einsetzen. Sie können sie auch als Motive für Postkarten auf Karton oder in digitaler Form, oder als Ausschmückung für Ihre Briefe, Flyer etc. verwenden.
Die Bilder lassen sich direkt in die meisten Zeichen-, Bildbearbeitungs-, Illustrations-, Textverarbeitungs- und E-Mail-Programme laden, ohne dass zusätzliche Programme installiert werden müssen. In einigen Programmen können die Dokumente direkt geladen werden, in anderen müssen Sie zuerst ein Dokument anlegen und können dann die Datei importieren. Genauere Hinweise dazu finden Sie im Handbuch zu Ihrer Software.
Die Namen der Bilddateien auf der CD-ROM entsprechen den Seitenzahlen dieses Buchs. Bei Seiten mit mehreren Bildern verläuft die Reihenfolge von links nach rechts und oben nach unten. Wo die Position auf der jeweiligen Seite angegeben ist, bedeutet T (top)= oben, B (bottom)= unten, C (centre)= Mitte, L (left)= links und R (right)= rechts.
Die CD-ROM wird kostenlos mit dem Buch geliefert und ist nicht separat verkäuflich. Der Verlag haftet nicht für Inkompatibilität der CD-ROM mit Ihrem System.
Für nicht professionelle Anwendungen können einzelne Bilder kostenfrei genutzt werden. Die Bilder dürfen ohne vorherige Genehmigung von The Pepin Press /Agile Rabbit Editions nicht für kommerzielle oder sonstige professionelle Anwendungen einschließlich aller Arten von gedruckten oder digitalen Medien eingesetzt werden.

Für Fragen zu Genehmigungen und Preisen wenden Sie sich bitte an:
mail@pepinpress.com
Fax +31 20 4201152

Français

Cet ouvrage renferme des illustrations destinées à servir de ressources graphiques ou d'inspiration. La totalité des images sont stockées en format haute définition sur le CD-ROM gratuit inclus (Mac et Windows), prêtes à l'emploi en vue de réaliser des impressions ou pages Web de qualité professionnelle. Elles permettent également de créer des cartes postales, aussi bien sur papier que virtuelles, ou d'agrémenter vos courriers, prospectus et autres.
Vous pouvez les importer directement à partir du CD dans la plupart des applications de création, manipulation graphique, illustration, traitement de texte et messagerie, sans qu'aucune installation ne soit nécessaire. Certaines applications permettent d'accéder directement aux images, tandis que dans d'autres, vous devez d'abord créer un document, puis importer les images. Veuillez consultez les instructions dans le manuel du logiciel concerné.
Sur le CD, les noms des fichiers correspondent aux numéros de pages de ce livre. Sur les pages qui comportent plusieurs images, l'ordre va de gauche à droite, et de haut en bas. Il est indiqué soit par un numéro figurant après le numéro de page, soit par les codes suivants : T (top)= haut, B (bottom)= bas, C (centre)= centre, L (left)= gauche, et R (right)= droite.
Le CD-ROM est fourni gratuitement avec le livre, mais il ne peut être vendu séparément. L'éditeur décline toute responsabilité si ce CD n'est pas compatible avec votre ordinateur.
Vous pouvez utiliser les images individuelles sans frais dans des applications non-professionnelles. Il est interdit d'utiliser les images avec des applications de type professionnel ou commercial (y compris toutes les sortes de publications numériques ou imprimés) sans l'autorisation préalable de The Pepin Press/Agile Rabbit Editions.

Pour tout renseignement relatif aux autorisations et aux frais d'utilisation:
mail@pepinpress.com
Fax +31 20 4201152

Italiano

Questo libro contiene immagini che possono essere utilizzate come risorsa grafica o come fonte di ispirazione. Tutte le illustrazioni sono contenute nell'allegato CD-ROM gratuito (per Mac e Windows), in formato ad alta risoluzione e pronte per essere utilizzate per pubblicazioni professionali e pagine web. Possono essere inoltre usate per creare cartoline, su carta o digitali, o per abbellire lettere, opuscoli, ecc.
Dal CD, le immagini possono essere importate direttamente nella maggior parte dei programmi di grafica, di ritocco, di illustrazione, di scrittura e di posta elettronica; non è richiesto alcun tipo di installazione. Alcuni programmi vi consentiranno di accedere alle immagini direttamente; in altri, invece, dovrete prima creare un documento e poi importare le immagini. Consultate il manuale del software per maggiori informazioni.
I nomi dei documenti sul CD-ROM corrispondono ai numeri delle pagine del libro. Quando le pagine contengono più di un'immagine, l'ordine di queste ultime è da sinistra a destra e dall'alto verso il basso. L'ordine è indicato con un numero situato dopo il numero di pagina o con le seguenti lettere: T (top)= alto, B (bottom)= basso, C (centre)= centro, L (left)= sinistra e R (right)= destra.
Il CD-ROM è allegato gratuitamente al libro e non può essere venduto separatamente. L'editore non può essere ritenuto responsabile qualora il CD non fosse compatibile con il sistema posseduto.
Per applicazioni di tipo non professionale, le singole immagini possono essere utilizzate gratuitamente. Se desiderate, invece, utilizzare le immagini per applicazioni di tipo professionale o con scopi commerciali, comprese tutte le pubblicazioni digitali o stampate, sarà necessaria la relativa autorizzazione da parte della casa editrice The Pepin Press/Agile Rabbit Editions.

Per ulteriori informazioni su autorizzazioni e canoni per il diritto di sfruttamento commerciale rivolgetevi a:
mail@pepinpress.com
Fax +31 20 4201152

Español

En este libro podrá encontrar imágenes que le servirán como fuente de material gráfico o como inspiración para realizar sus propios diseños. Se adjunta un CD-ROM gratuito (Mac y Windows) donde hallará todas las ilustraciones en un formato de alta resolución, con las que podrá conseguir una impresión de calidad profesional y diseñar páginas web. Las imágenes pueden también emplearse para realizar postales, de papel o digitales, o para decorar cartas, folletos, etc.
Estas imágenes se pueden importar desde el CD a la mayoría de programas de diseño, manipulación de imágenes, dibujo, tratamiento de textos y correo electrónico, sin necesidad de utilizar un programa de instalación. Algunos programas le permitirán acceder a las imágenes directamente; otros, sin embargo, requieren la creación previa de un documento para importar las imágenes. Consulte su manual de software en caso de duda.
Los nombres de los archivos del CD-ROM se corresponden con los números de página de este libro. En aquellas páginas en las que haya más de una imagen, el orden que se ha de seguir para localizarlas es de izquierda a derecha y de arriba abajo. Esto se indica con un número a continuación del número de página, o con las siguientes abreviaturas: T (top)= arriba; B (bottom)= abajo; C (centre)= centro; L (left)= izquierda y R (right)= derecha.
El CD-ROM se ofrece de manera gratuita con este libro, pero está prohibida su venta por separado. Los editores no asumen ninguna responsabilidad en el caso de que el CD no sea compatible con su sistema.
Se autoriza el uso de estas imágenes de manera gratuita para aplicaciones no profesionales. No se podrán emplear en aplicaciones de tipo profesional o comercial (incluido cualquier tipo de publicación impresa o digital) sin la autorización previa de The Pepin Press/Agile Rabbit Editions.

Para más información acerca de autorizaciones y tarifas:
mail@pepinpress.com
Fax +31 20 4201152

Português

Este livro contém imagens que podem ser utilizadas como fonte de material gráfico ou como inspiração para realizar os seus próprios desenhos. Você encontrará todas as ilustrações em formato de alta resolução dentro do CD-ROM gratuito (Mac e Windows), e com elas poderá conseguir uma impressão de qualidade profissional e desenhar páginas web. As imagens também podem ser usadas para criar postais, de papel ou digitais, ou para decorar cartas, folhetos, etc.
Estas imagens podem ser importadas do CD para a maioria de programas de desenho, manipulação de imagem, ilustração, processamento de texto e correio eletrônico, sem a necessidade de utilizar um programa de instalação. Alguns programas permitirão que você tenha acesso às imagens diretamente; e em outros, você deverá criar um documento antes de importar as imagens. Por favor, consulte o seu manual de software para obter maiores informações.
Os nomes dos arquivos do CD-ROM correspondem aos números de página deste livro. Nas páginas onde exista mais de uma imagem, a ordem que deve ser seguida para localizar as imagens é da esquerda para a direita e de cima para baixo. Isso é indicado com um número que vem logo depois do número de página, ou com as seguintes abreviaturas: T (top)= acima; B (bottom)= abaixo; C (centre)= centro; L (left)= esquerda e R (right)= direita.
O CD-ROM é oferecido de forma gratuita com este livro, porém é proibido vendê-lo separadamente. Os editores não assumem nenhuma responsabilidade no caso de que o CD não seja compatível com o seu sistema.
Desde que não seja para aplicação profissional, as imagens individuais podem ser utilizadas gratuitamente. As imagens não podem ser empregadas em nenhum tipo de aplicação comercial ou profissional – incluindo todos os tipos de publicações impressas ou digitais – sem a prévia permissão de The Pepin Press/Agile Rabbit Editions.

Para esclarecer dúvidas a respeito das permissões e taxas:
mail@pepinpress.com
Fax +31 20 4201152

日本語

本書にはグラフィック リソースやインスピレーションとして使用できる美しいイメージ画像が含まれています。すべてのイラストレーションは、無料の付属 CD-ROM（Mac および Windows 用）に高解像度で保存されており、これらを利用してプロ品質の印刷物や WEB ページを簡単に作成することができます。また、紙ベースまたはデジタルの葉書の作成やレター、ちらしの装飾等に使用することもできます。

これらの画像は、CD から主なデザイン、画像処理、イラスト、ワープロ、E メールソフトウェアに直接取り込むことができます。インストレーションは必要ありません。プログラムによっては、画像に直接アクセスできる場合や、一旦ドキュメントを作成した後に画像を取り込む場合等があります。詳細は、ご使用のソフトウェアのマニュアルをご参照下さい。

CD-ROM 上のファイル名は、本書のページ数に対応しています。ページに複数の画像が含まれる場合は、左から右、上から下の順番で番号がつけられ、ページ番号に続く数字または下記のレターコードで識別されます。

T = トップ（上部）、B = ボトム（下部）、C = センター（中央）、L = レフト（左）、R = ライト（右）

CD-ROM は本書の付属品であり、別売されておりません。CD がお客様のシステムと互換でなかった場合、発行者は責任を負わないことをご了承下さい。

プロ用以外のアプリケーションで、画像を一回のみ無料で使用することができます。The Pepin Press / Agile Rabbit Editions から事前許可を得ることなく、あらゆる形体の印刷物、デジタル出版物をはじめとする、あらゆる種類の商業用ならびにプロ用アプリケーションで画像を使用することを禁止します。

使用許可と料金については、下記までお問い合わせ下さい。

mail@pepinpress.com
ファックス： +31 20 4201152

中 文

本書包含精美圖片，可以作為圖片資源或激發靈感的資料使用。這些圖片存儲在所附的高清晰度免費 CD-ROM (可在 Mac 和 Windows 下使用) 中，可用於專業的高品質印刷媒體和網頁設計。圖片還可以用於製作紙質和數字明信片，或裝飾您的信封、傳單等。您無需安裝即可以把圖片直接從 CD 調入大多數的設計、圖像處理、圖片、文字處理和電子郵件程序。有些程序允許您直接使用圖片；另外一些，您則需要先創建一個文件，然後引入圖片。用法說明請參閱軟體說明書。

在 CD 中的文件名稱是與書中的頁碼相對應的。如果書頁中的圖片超過一幅，其順序為從左到右，從上到下。這會在書頁號後加一個數字來表示，或者是加一個字母：T = 上，B = 下，C = 中，L = 左，R = 右。

本書附帶的 CD-ROM 是免費的，但 CD-ROM 不單獨出售。如果 CD 與您的系統不相容，出版商不承擔任何責任。

就非專業的用途而言，可以免費使用單個圖片。若未事先得到 The Pepin Press/Agile Rabbit Editions 的許可，不得將圖片用於任何其他類型的商業或專業用途 - 包括所有類型的印刷或數字出版物。

有關許可及收費的詢問，請查詢：

Mail@pepinpress.com
傳真： +31 20 4201152

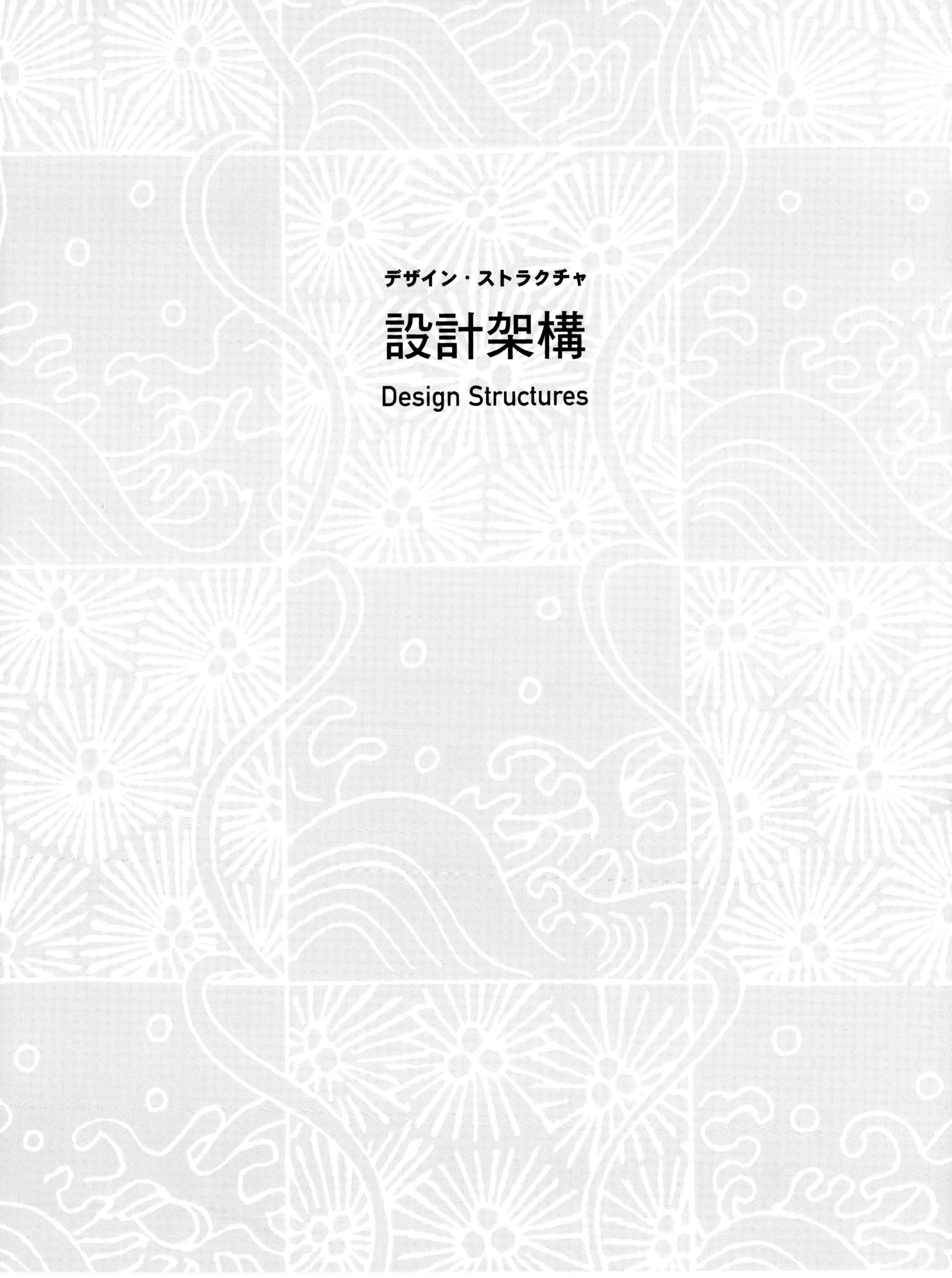

デザイン・ストラクチャ

設計架構

Design Structures

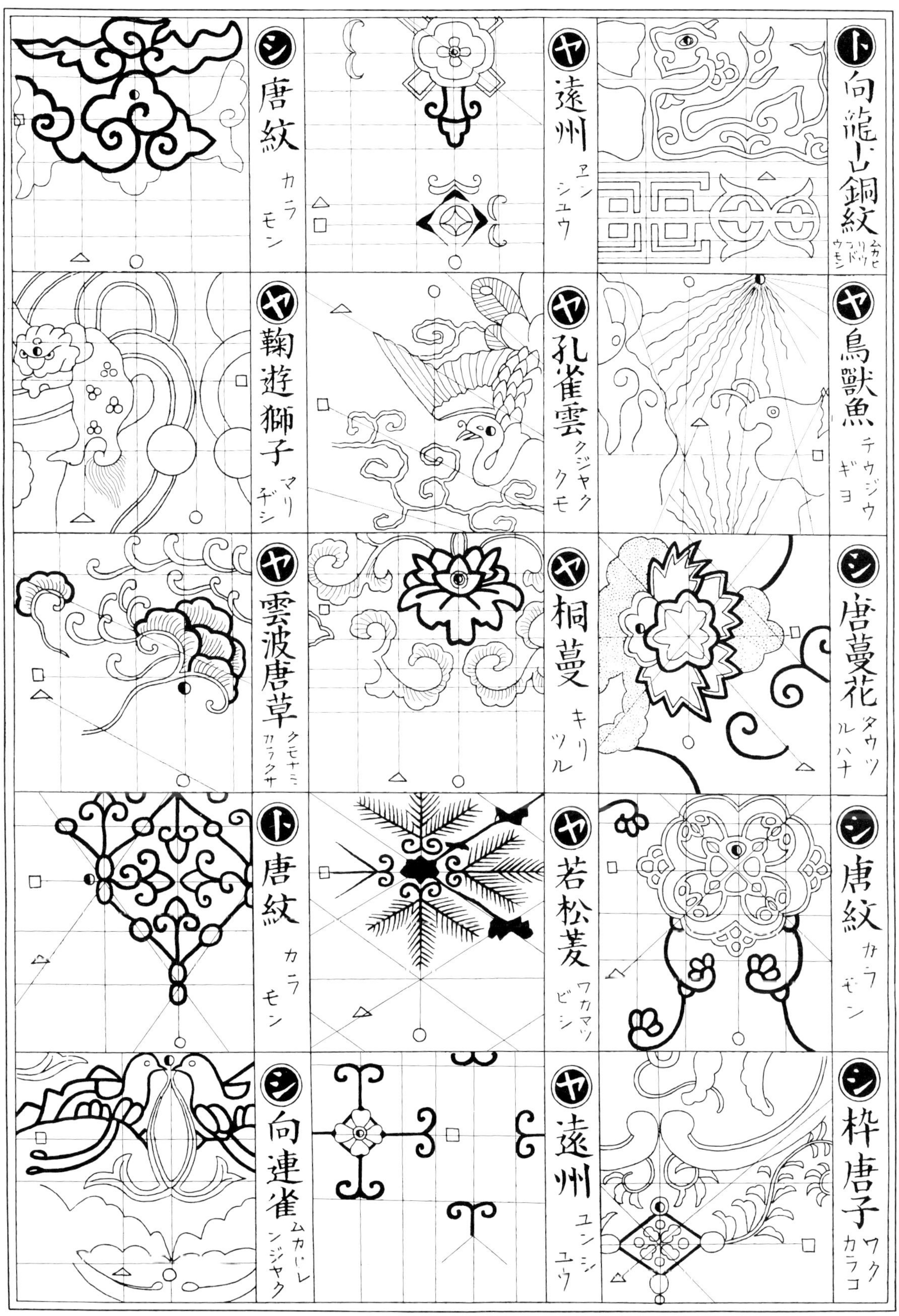
ト
向箆山銅紋
ヤ
遠州
エンシュウ
シ
唐紋
カラモン
ヤ
鳥獣魚
テウジウギヨ
ヤ
孔雀雲
クジヤククモ
ヤ
鞠遊獅子
マリチシ
シ
唐蔓花
タウツルハナ
ヤ
桐蔓
キリツル
ヤ
雲波唐草
クモナミカラクサ
シ
唐紋
カラモン
ヤ
若松菱
ワカマツビシ
ト
唐紋
カラモン
シ
枠唐子
ワクカラコ
ヤ
遠州
ユンシユウ
シ
向連雀
ムカヒレンジヤク

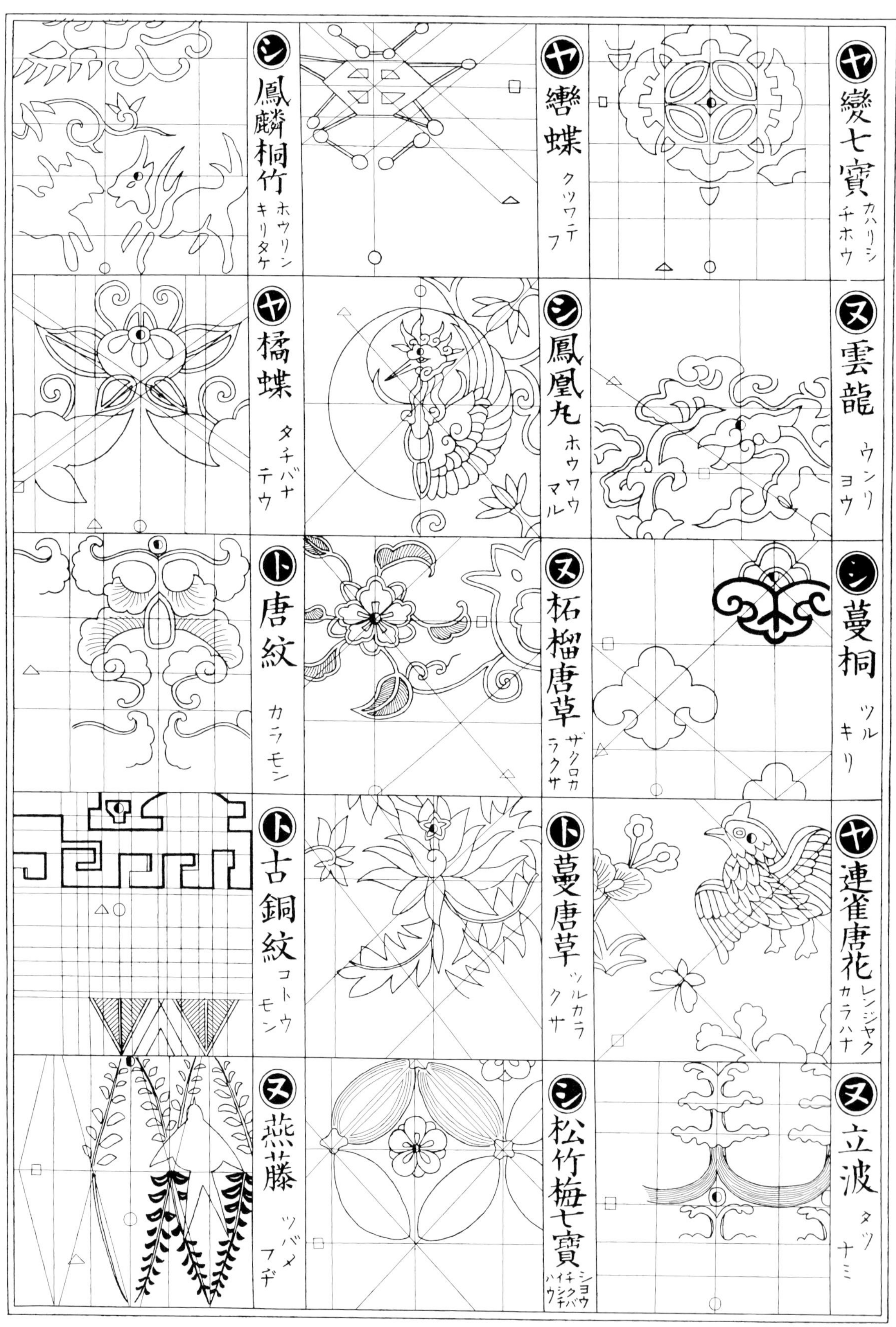

ヤ
變七寶
カハリシチホウ
ヤ
轡蝶
クツワテフ
シ
鳳麟桐竹
ホウリンキリタケ
ヌ
雲龍
ウンリヨウ
シ
鳳凰丸
ホウワウマル
ヤ
橘蝶
タチバナテウ
シ
蔓桐
ツルキリ
ヌ
柘榴唐草
ザクロカラクサ
ト
唐紋
カラモン
ヤ
連雀唐花
レンジヤクカラハナ
ト
蔓唐草
ツルカラクサ
ト
古銅紋
コトウモン
ヌ
立波
タツナミ
シ
松竹梅七寶
シヨウチクバイシチハウ
ヌ
燕藤
ツバメフヂ

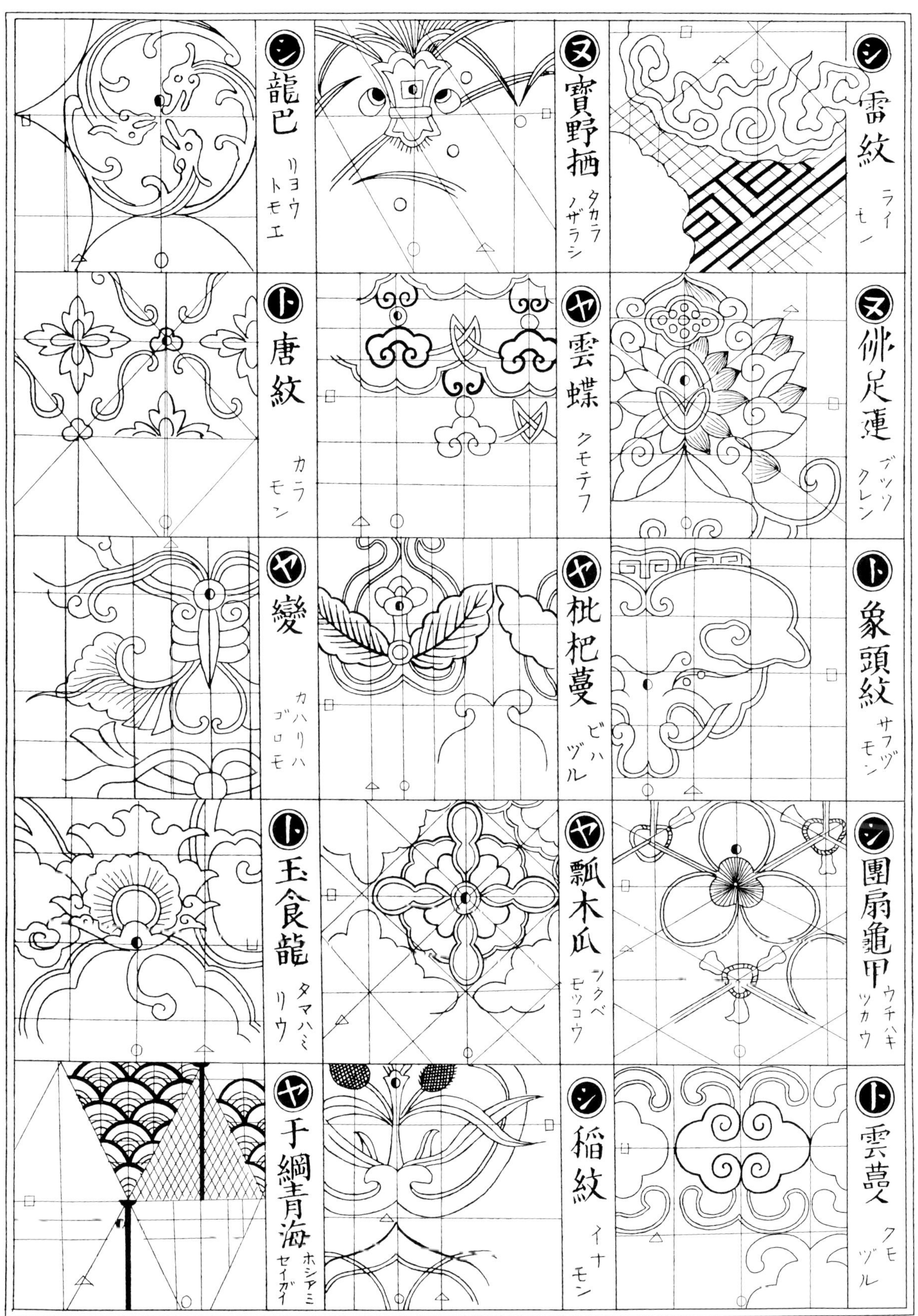

シ
龍巴
リヨウトモヱ
ヌ
寶野栖
タカラノザラシ
シ
雷紋
ライモン
ト
唐紋
カラモン
ヤ
雲蝶
クモテフ
ヌ
佛足蓮
ブツソクレン
ヤ
變
カハリハゴロモ
ヤ
枇杷蔓
ビハヅル
ト
象頭紋
サフヅモン
ト
玉食龍
タマハミリウ
ヤ
瓢木瓜
フクベモッコウ
シ
團扇龜甲
ウチハキツカウ
ヤ
干綱青海
ホシアミセイガイ
シ
稲紋
イナモン
ト
雲蔓
クモヅル

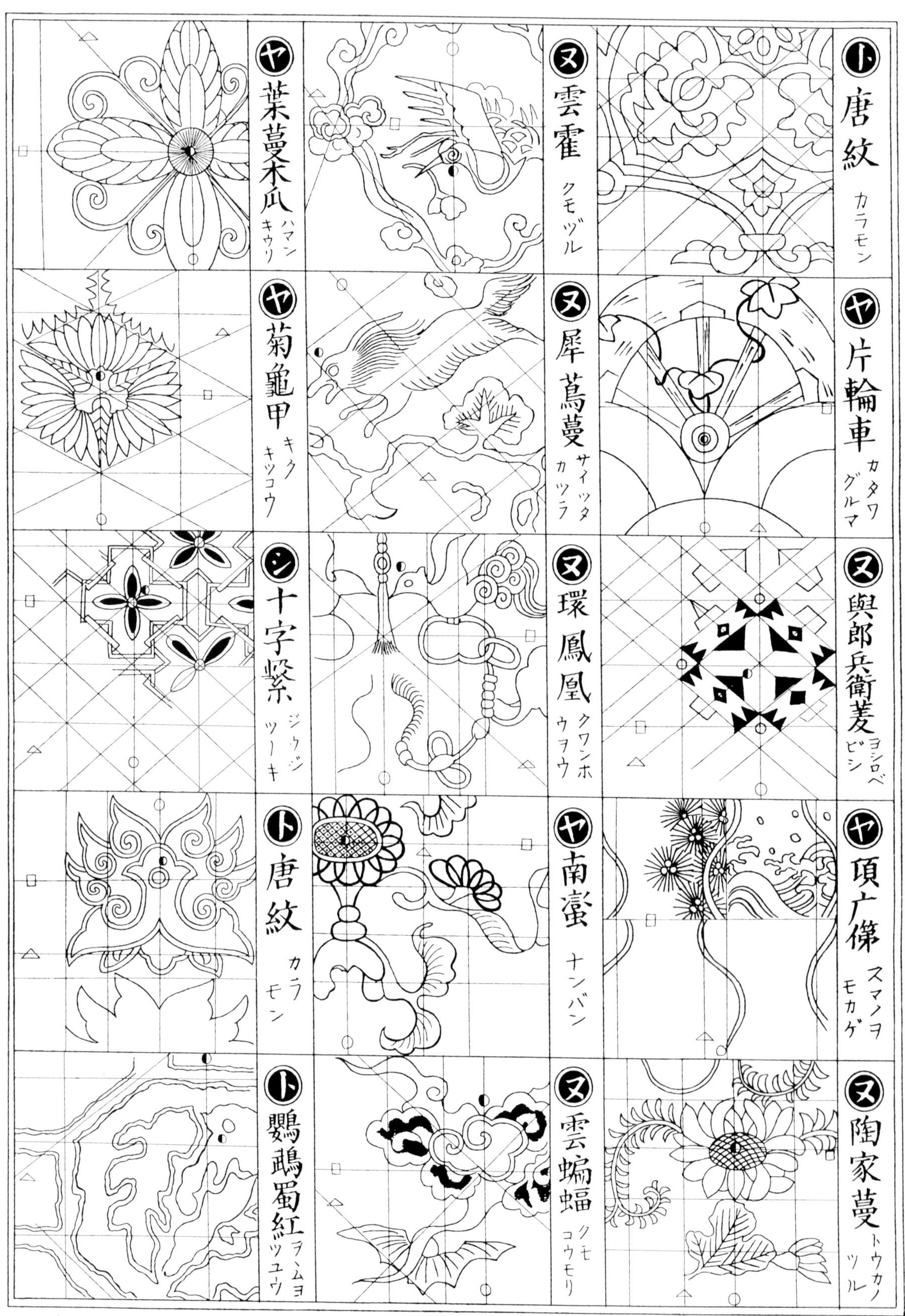

ト 唐紋 カラモン
ヌ 雲霍 クモヅル
ヤ 葉蔓木瓜 ハマンキウリ
ヤ 片輪車 カタワグルマ
ヌ 犀蔦蔓 サイツタカツラ
ヤ 菊龜甲 キクキツコウ
ヌ 與郎兵衛菱 ヨシロベビシ
ヌ 環鳳凰 クワンホウヲウ
シ 十字緊 ジウジツーキ
ヤ 頁广俤 スマノヲモカゲ
ヤ 南蛮 ナンバン
ト 唐紋 カラモン
ヌ 陶家蔓 トウカノツル
ヌ 雲蝙蝠 クモコウモリ
ト 鸚鵡蜀紅 ヲヽムヨツユウ

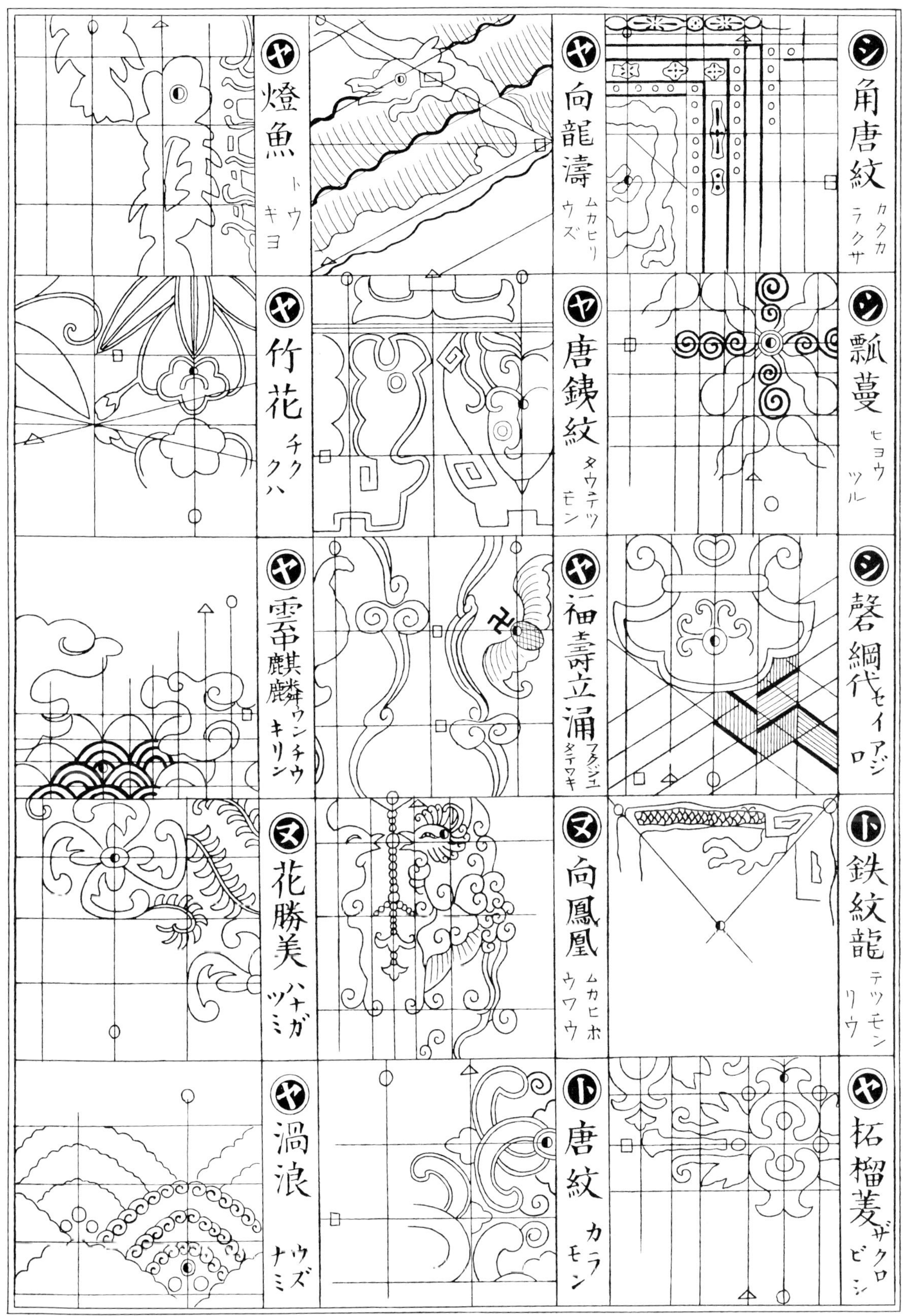

シ
角唐紋
カクカラクサ
ヤ
向龍濤
ムカヒリウズ
ヤ
燈魚
トウキヨ
シ
瓢蔓
ヒヨウツル
ヤ
唐鋳紋
タウテツモン
ヤ
竹花
チククハ
シ
磬綱代
セイアジロ
ヤ
福壽立涌
フクジユタテワキ
ヤ
雲中麒麟
ウンチウキリン
ト
鉄紋龍
テツモンリウ
ヌ
向鳳凰
ムカヒホウワウ
ヌ
花勝美
ハナガツミ
ヤ
柘榴菱
ザクロビシ
ト
唐紋
カラモン
ヤ
渦浪
ウズナミ

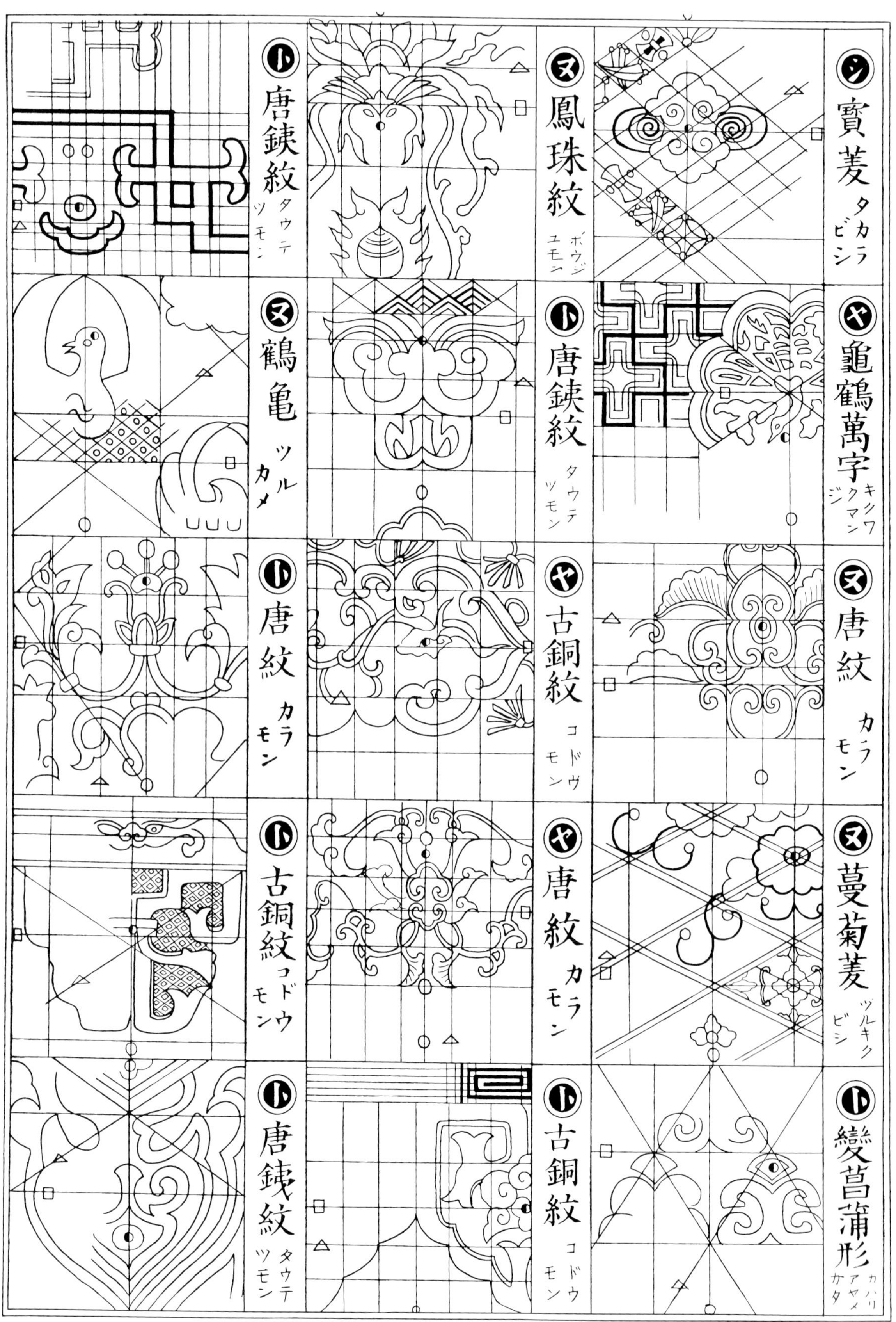
シ
寶菱
タカラビシ
ヌ
鳳珠紋
ボウジユモン
ト
唐銕紋
タウテツモン
ヤ
龜鶴萬字
キクワクマンジ
ト
唐銕紋
タウテツモン
ヌ
鶴亀
ツルカメ
ヌ
唐紋
カラモン
ヤ
古銅紋
コドウモン
ト
唐紋
カラモン
ヌ
蔓菊菱
ツルキクビシ
ヤ
唐紋
カラモン
ト
古銅紋
コドウモン
ト
變菖蒲形
カハリアヤメカタ
ト
古銅紋
コドウモン
ト
唐銕紋
タウテツモン

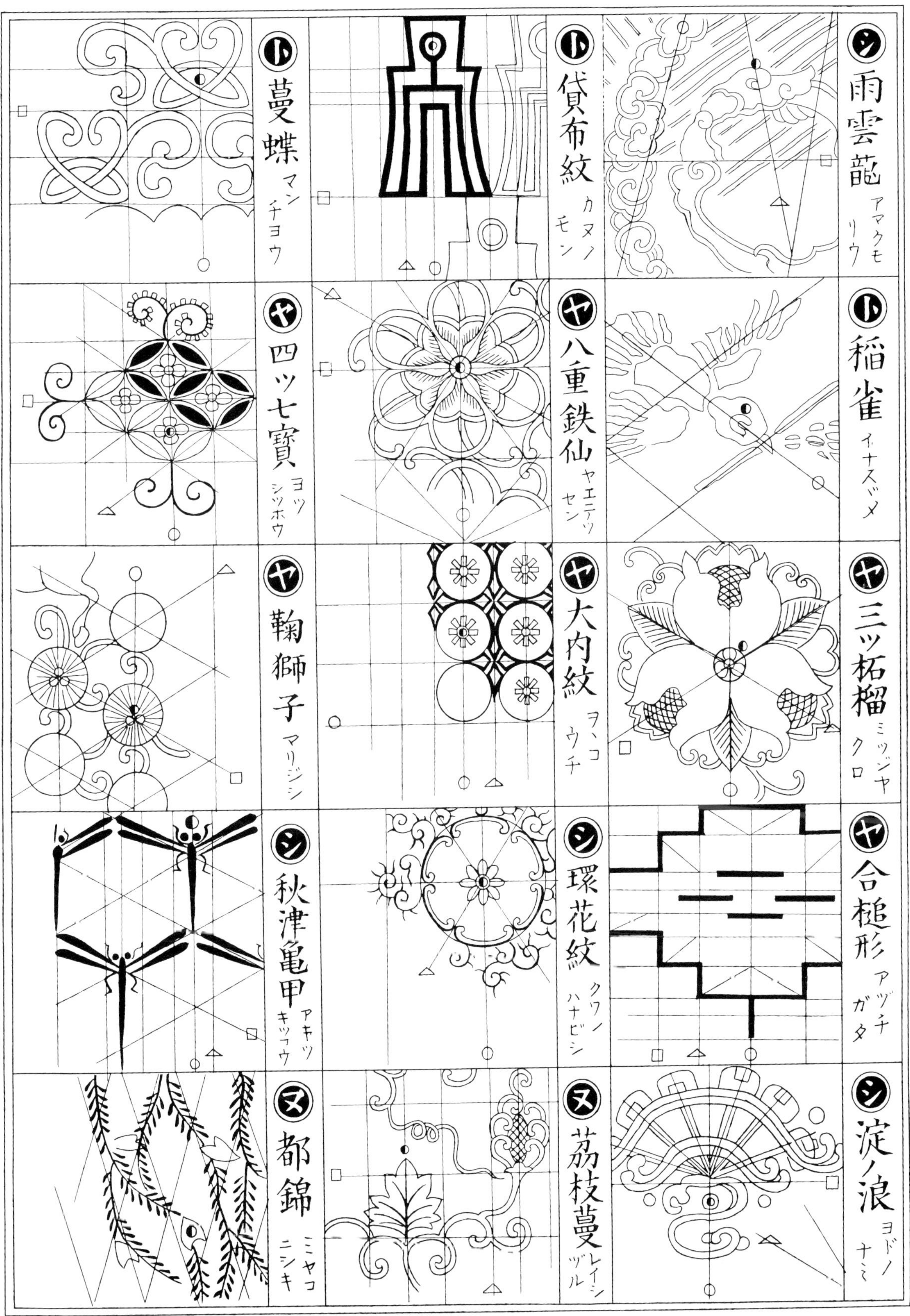

シ
雨雲龍
アマクモリウ
ト
貸布紋
カヌノモン
ト
蔓蝶
マンチヨウ
ト
稲雀
イナスズメ
ヤ
八重鉄仙
ヤエテツセン
ヤ
四ツ七寳
ヨツシツホウ
ヤ
三ツ柘榴
ミツジヤクロ
ヤ
大内紋
ヲヽコウチ
ヤ
鞠獅子
マリジシ
ヤ
合槌形
アヅチガタ
シ
環花紋
クワンハナビシ
シ
秋津亀甲
アキツキッコウ
シ
淀ノ浪
ヨドノナミ
ヌ
茘枝蔓
レイシヅル
ヌ
都錦
ミヤコニシキ

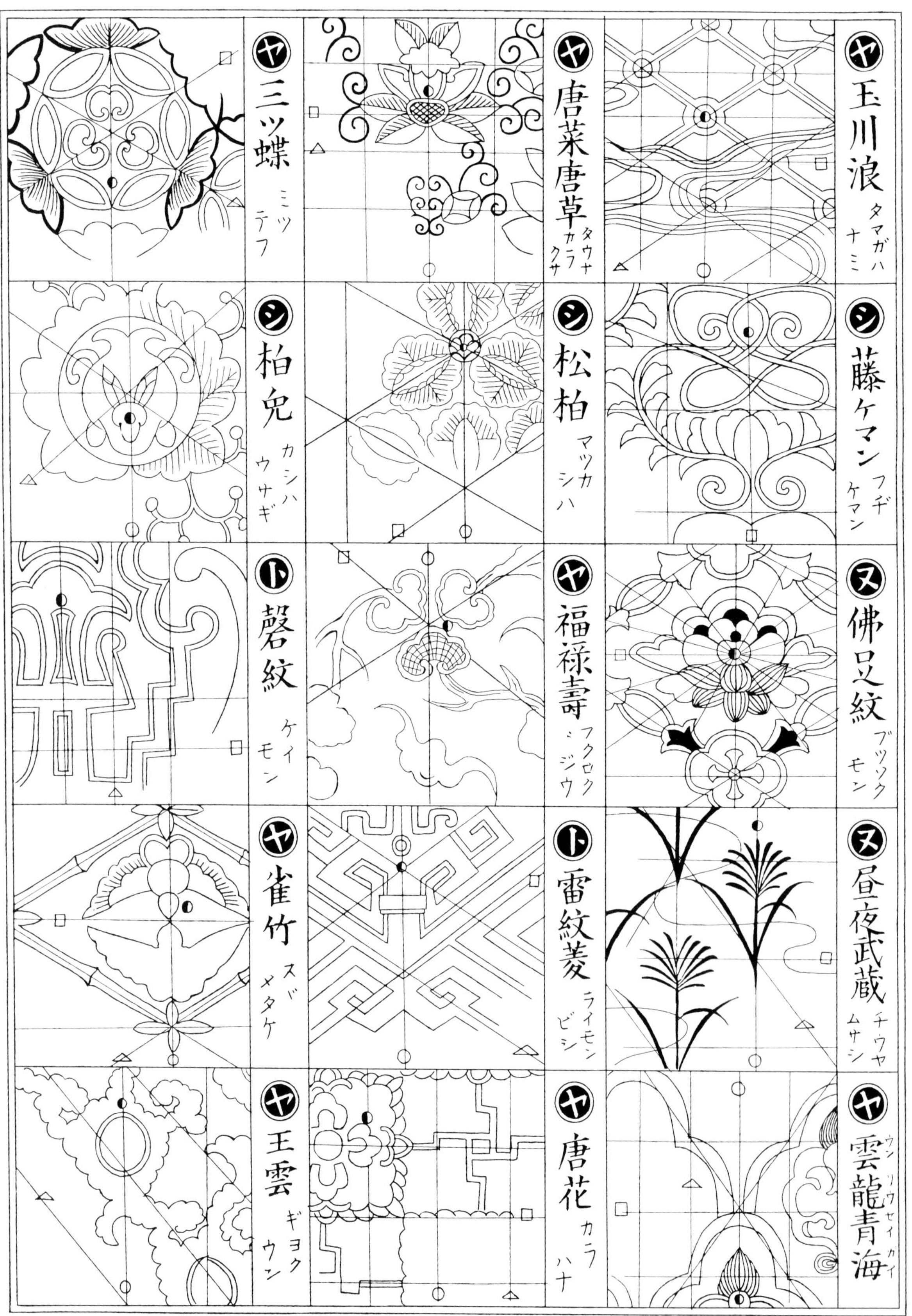

ヤ
玉川浪
タマガハナミ
ヤ
唐菜唐草
タウナカラクサ
ヤ
三ツ蝶
ミツテフ
シ
藤ケマン
フヂケマン
シ
松柏
マツカシハ
シ
柏兎
カシハウサギ
ヌ
佛足紋
ブツソクモン
ヤ
福禄壽
フクロクジウ
ト
磬紋
ケイモン
ヌ
昼夜武蔵
チウヤムサシ
ト
雷紋菱
ライモンビシ
ヤ
雀竹
スヾメタケ
ヤ
雲龍青海
ウンリウセイカイ
ヤ
唐花
カラハナ
ヤ
王雲
ギヨクウン

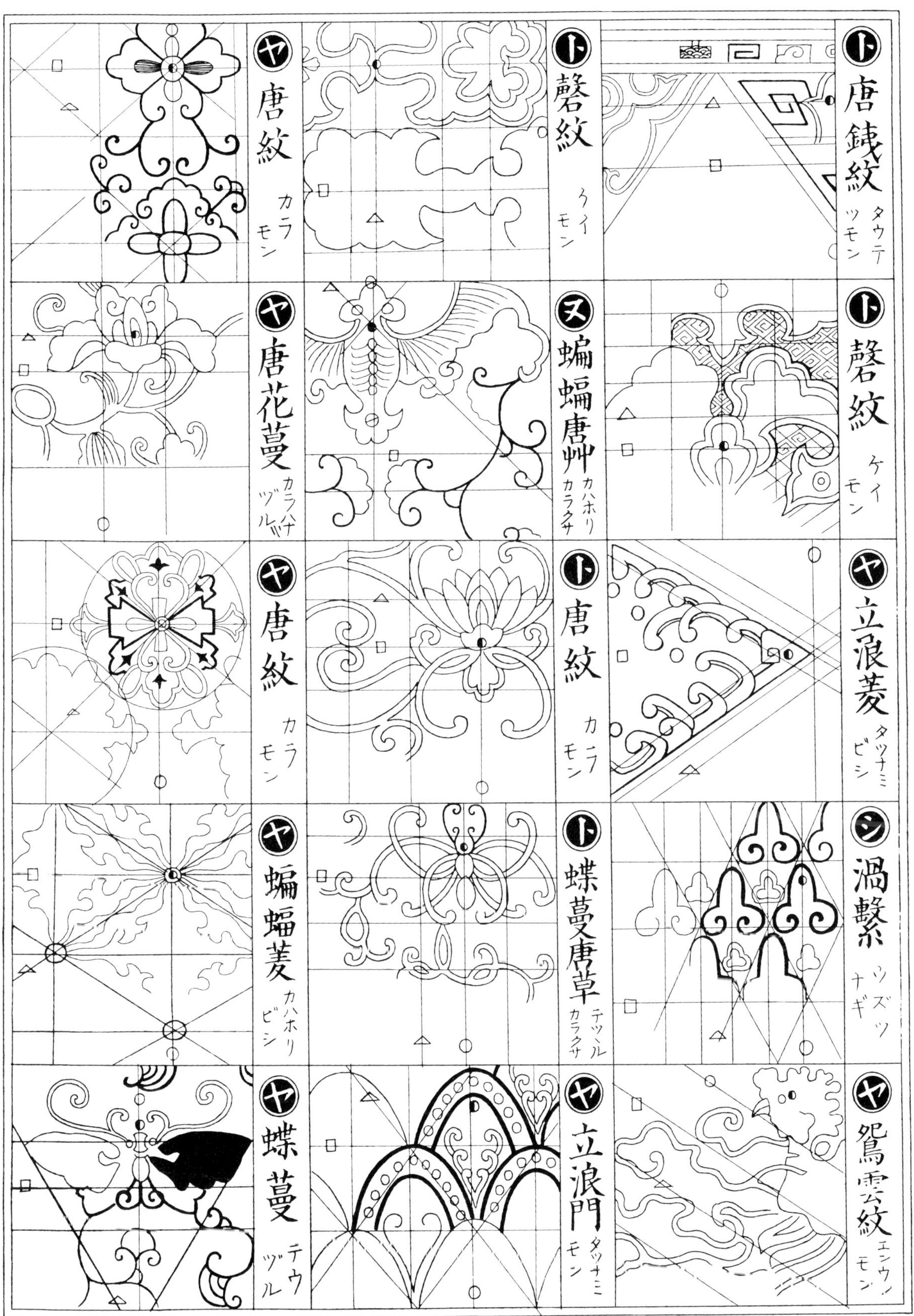
ト
唐銭紋
タウテツモン
ト
磬紋
ケイモン
ヤ
唐紋
カラモン
ト
磬紋
ケイモン
ヌ
蝙蝠唐艸
カハホリカラクサ
ヤ
唐花蔓
カラハナヅル
ヤ
立浪菱
タツナミビシ
ト
唐紋
カラモン
ヤ
唐紋
カラモン
シ
渦繋
ウズツナギ
ト
蝶蔓唐草
テツヽルカラクサ
ヤ
蝙蝠菱
カハホリビシ
ヤ
鴛雲紋
エンウンモン
ヤ
立浪門
タツナミモン
ヤ
蝶蔓
テウヅル

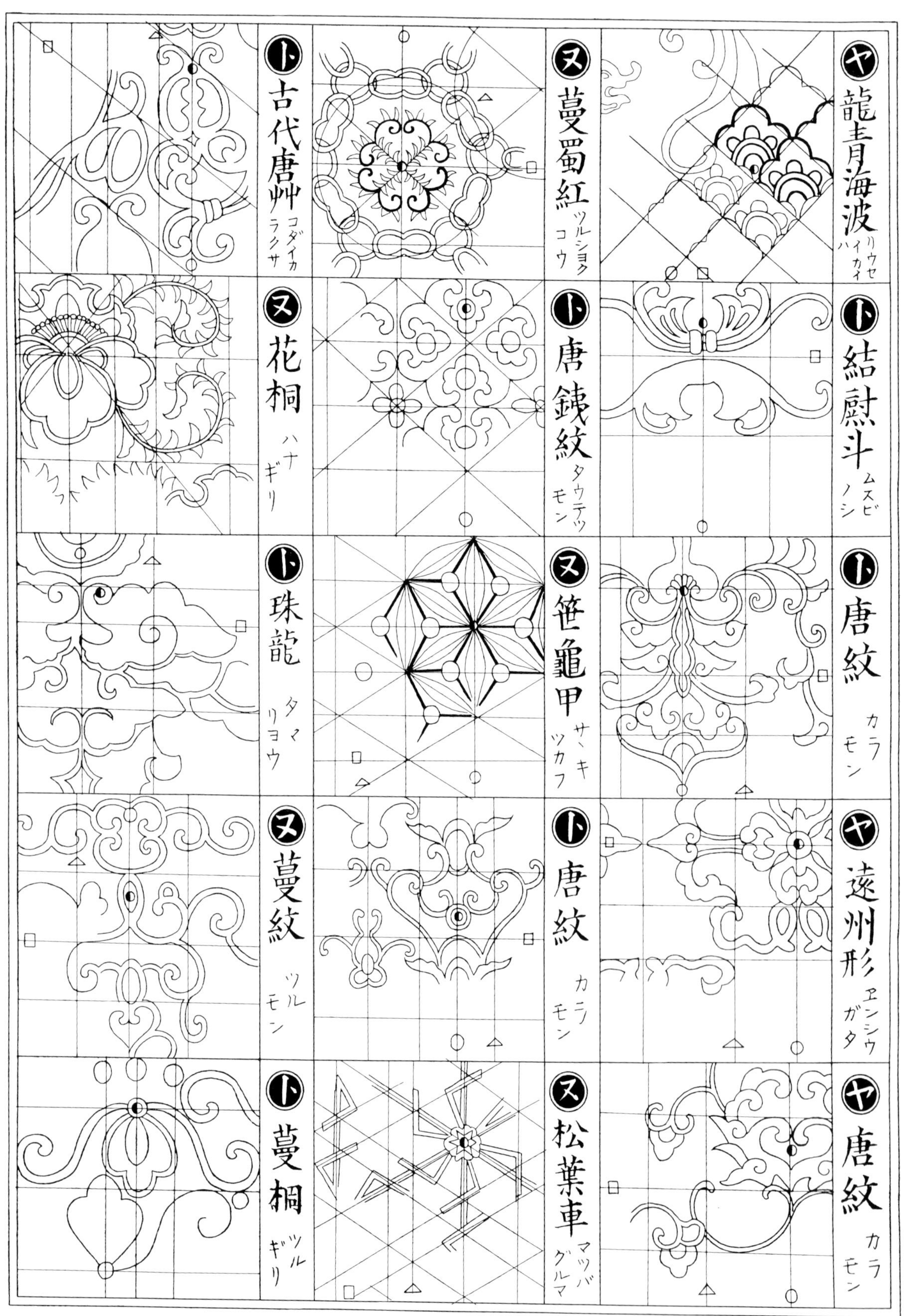

ヤ
龍青海波
リウセイカイハ
ヌ
蔓蜀紅
ツルショクコウ
ト
古代唐艸
コダイカラクサ
ト
結熨斗
ムスビノシ
ト
唐錢紋
タウテツモン
ヌ
花桐
ハナギリ
ト
唐紋
カラモン
ヌ
笹亀甲
サヽキツカフ
ト
珠龍
タマリヨウ
ヤ
遠州形
ヱンシウガタ
ト
唐紋
カラモン
ヌ
蔓紋
ツルモン
ヤ
唐紋
カラモン
ヌ
松葉車
マツバグルマ
ト
蔓桐
ツルギリ

デザイン
設計
Designs

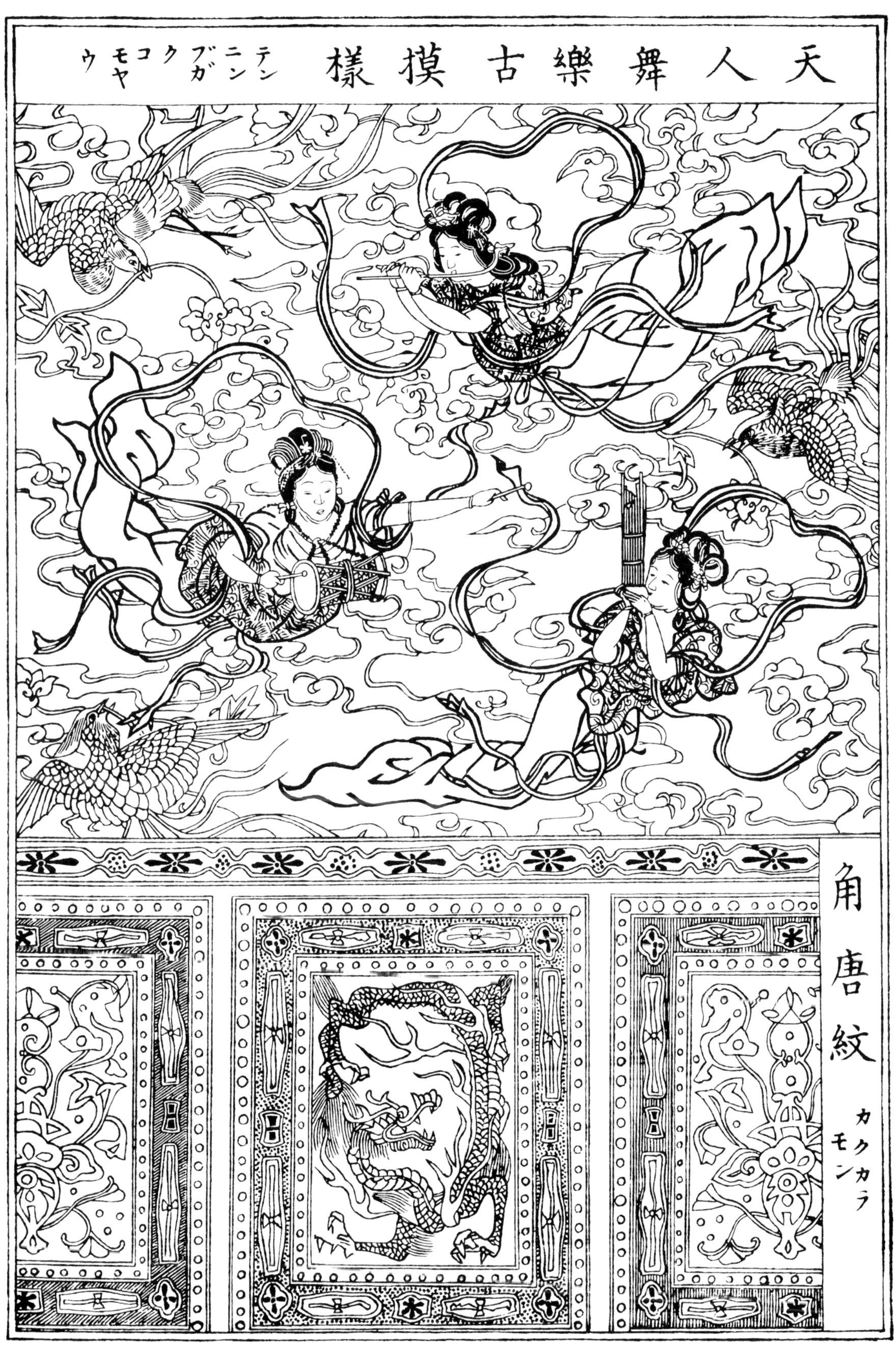
天人舞樂古模樣
テンニンブガクコモヤウ
角唐紋
カクカラモン

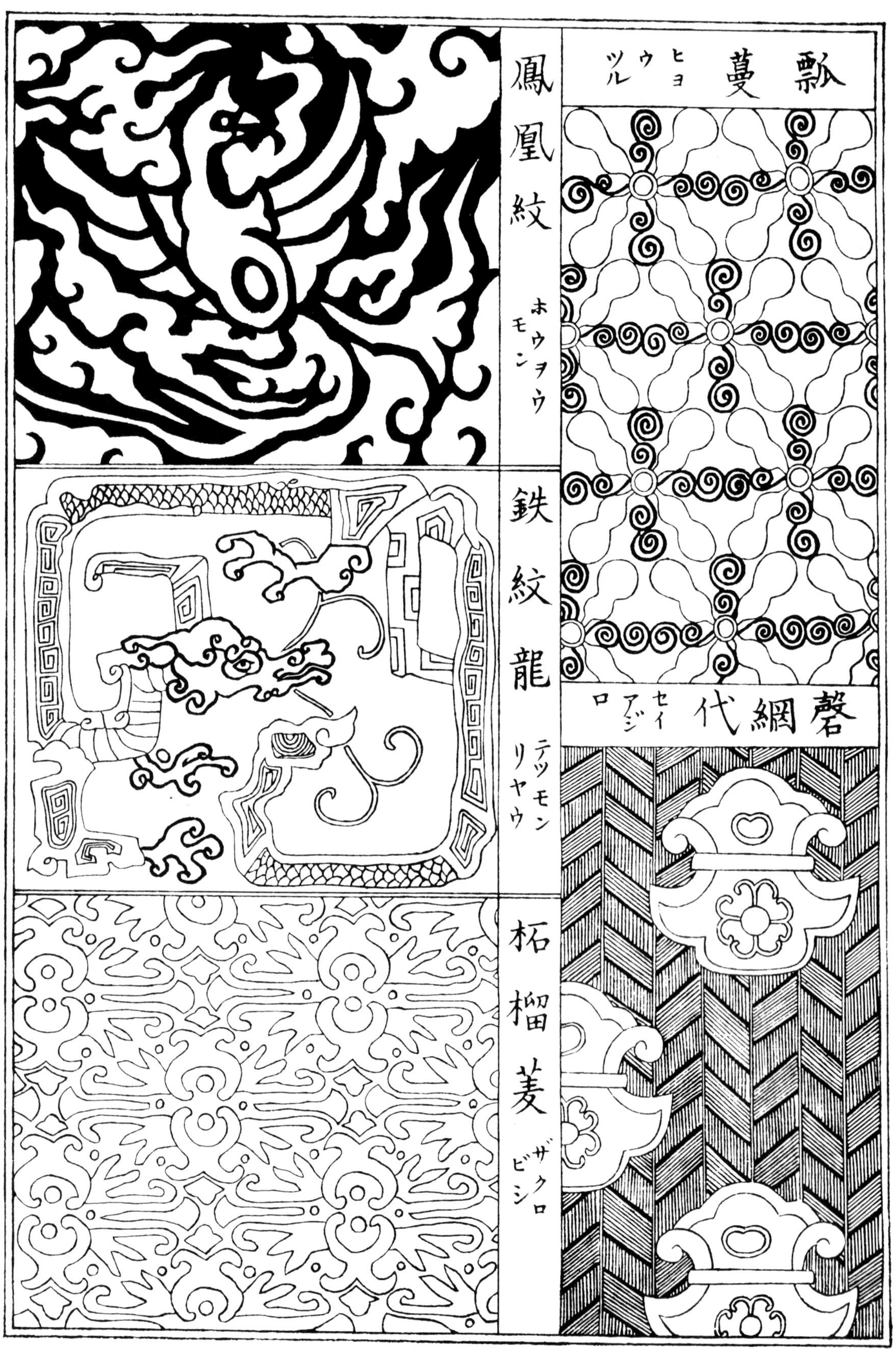

鳳凰紋
ホウヲウモン
瓢蔓
ヒョウツル
鉄紋龍
テツモンリヤウ
磬綱代
セイアジロ
柘榴菱
ザクロビシ

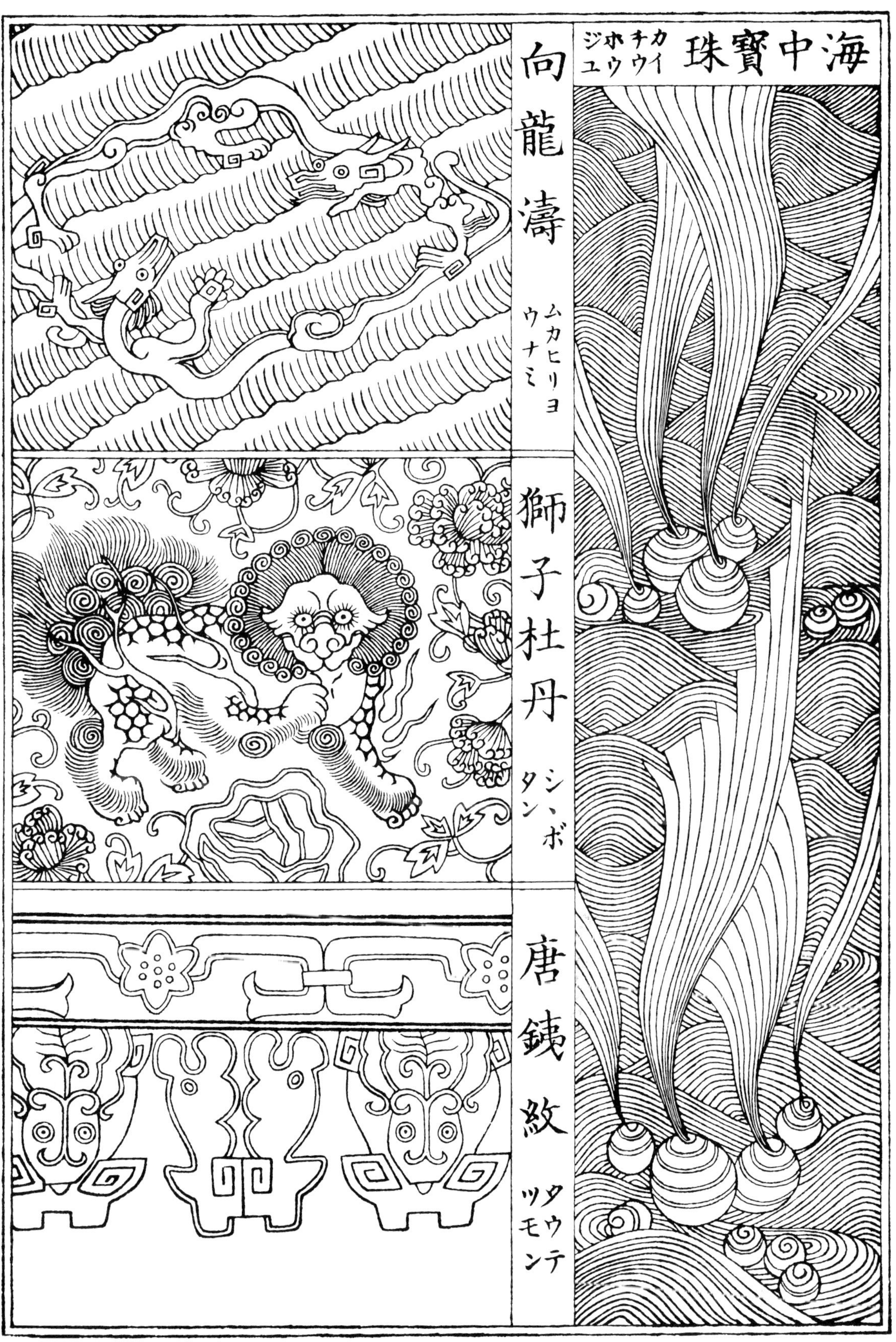

海中寶珠
カイチウホウジユ
向龍濤
ムカヒリヨウナミ
獅子杜丹
シヽボタン
唐銕紋
タウテツモン

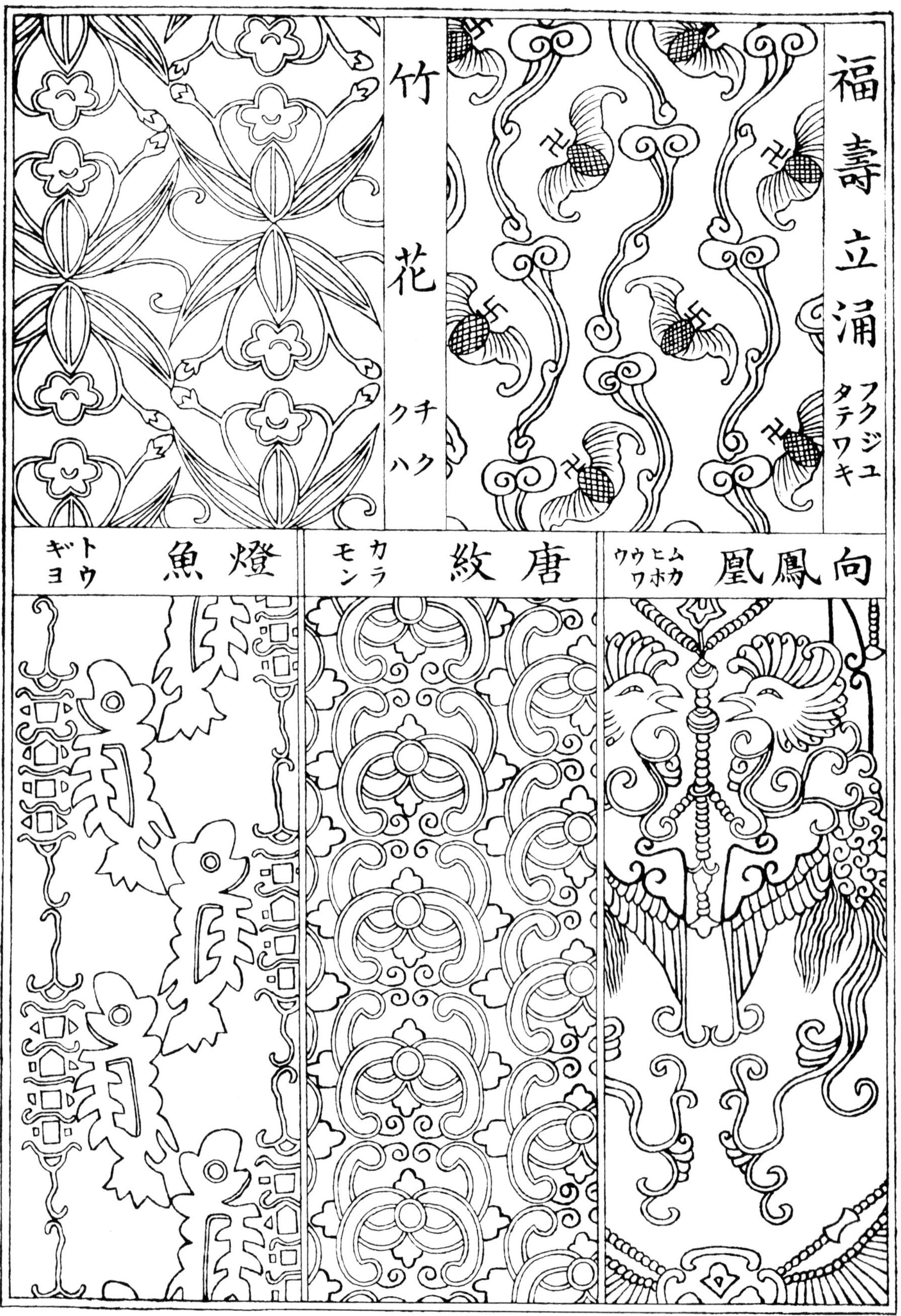

福壽立涌
フクジユ タテワキ
竹花
チク クハ
向鳳凰
ムカヒ ホウワウ
唐紋
カラ モン
燈魚
トウ ギヨ

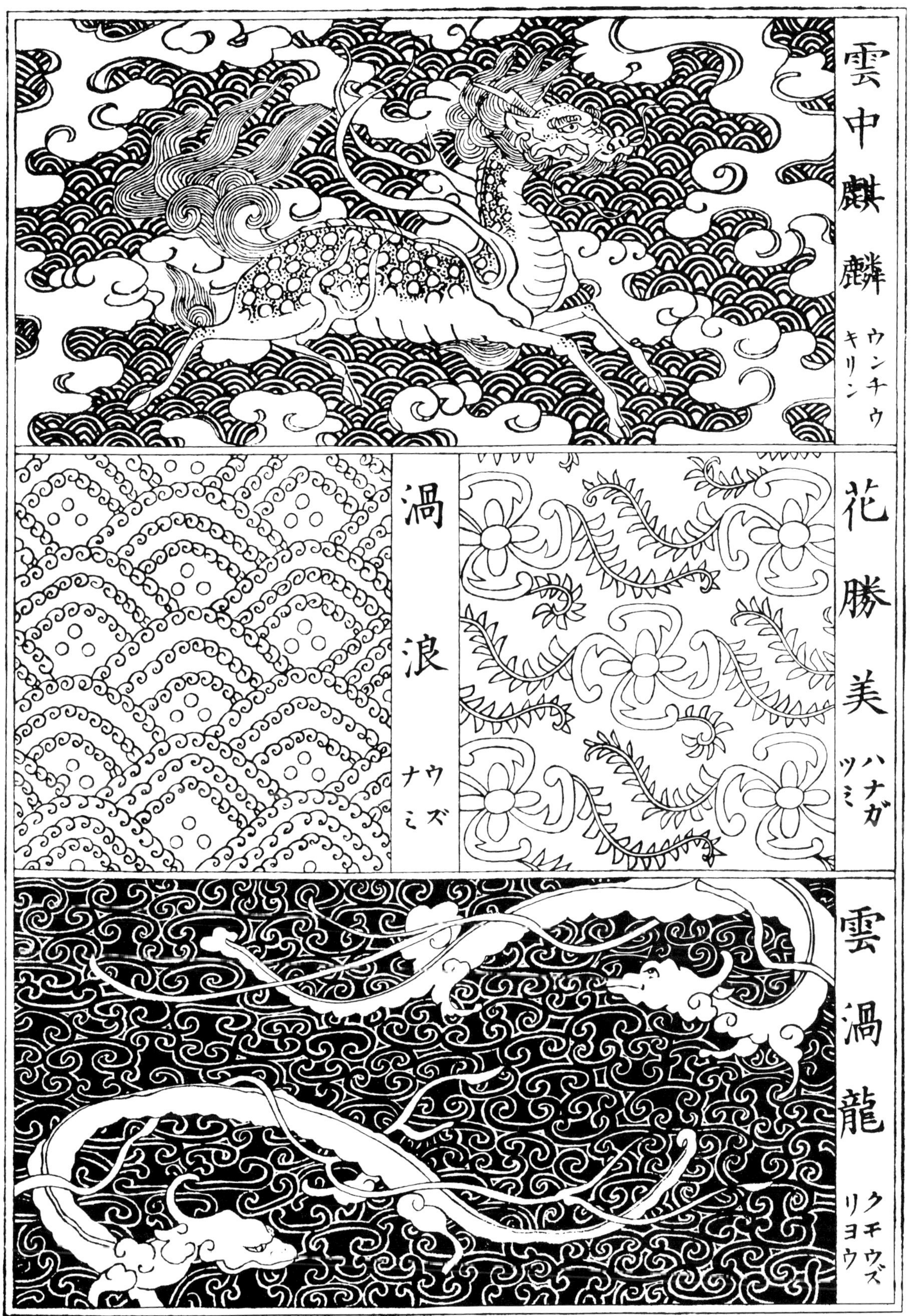

雲中麒麟
ウンチウキリン
花勝美
ハナガツミ
渦浪
ウズナミ
雲渦龍
クモウズリヨウ

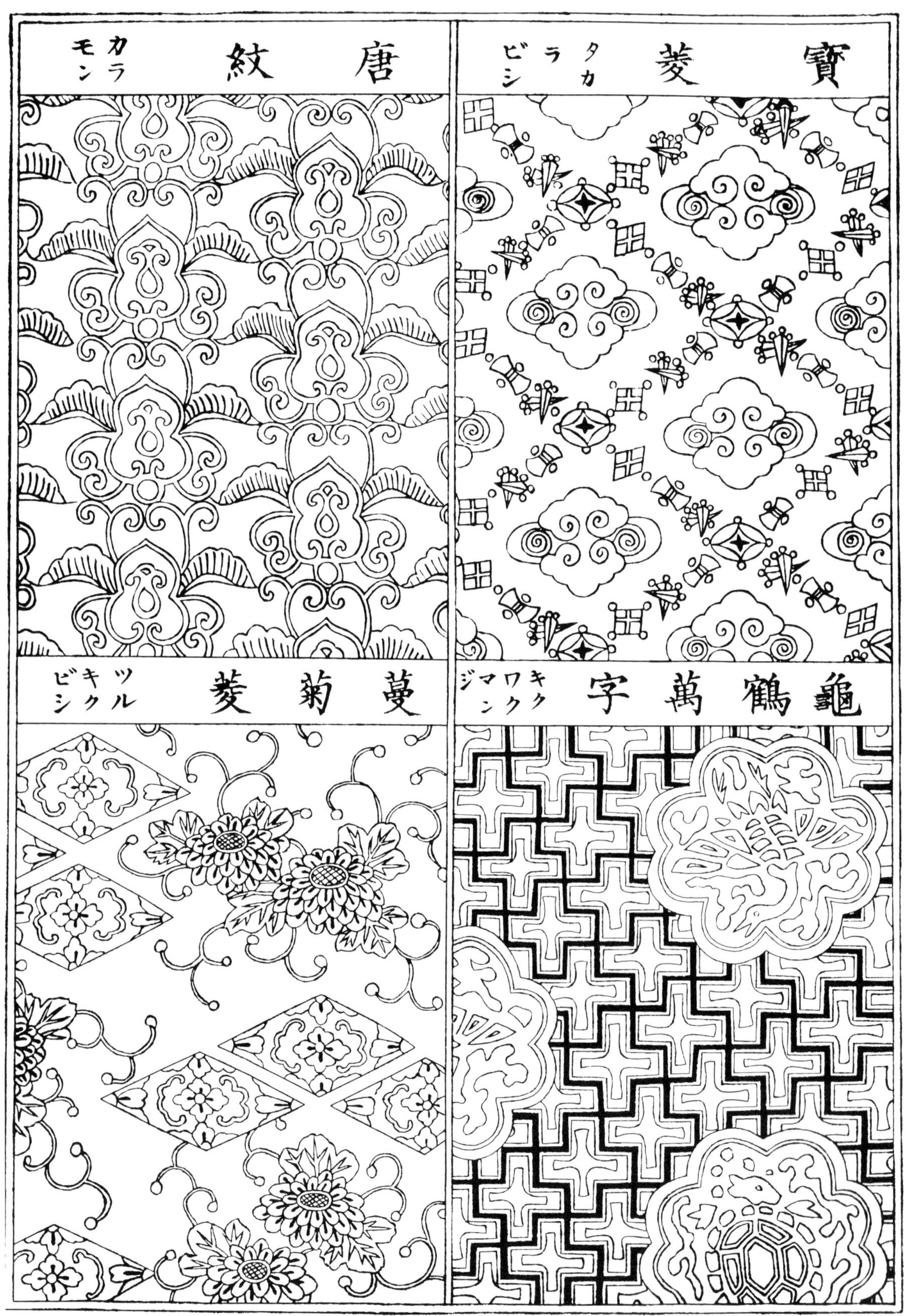
唐紋
カラモン
寶菱
タカラビシ
蔓菊菱
ツルキクビシ
龜鶴萬字
キクワクマンジ

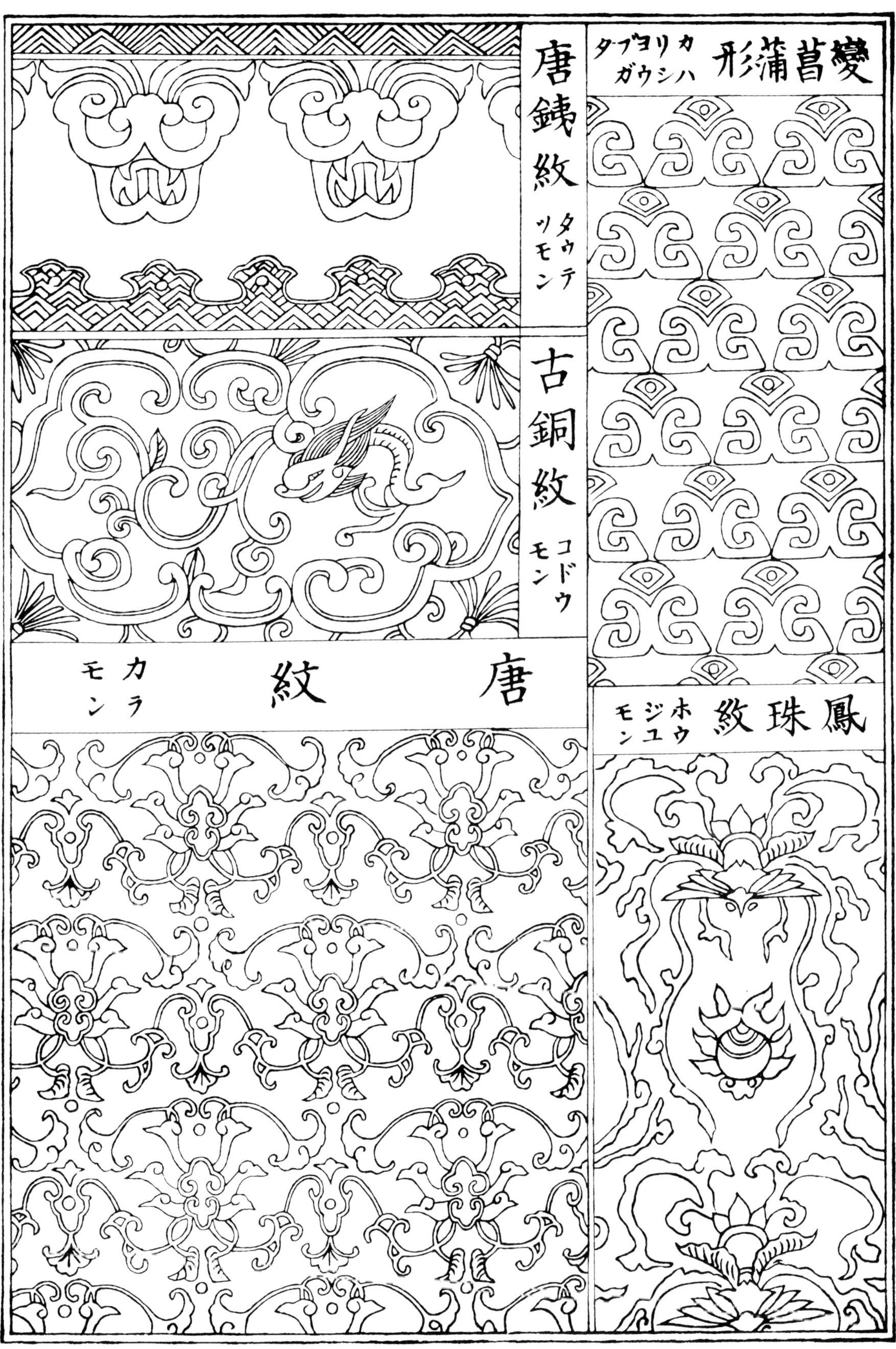
變菖蒲形
カハリシヨウブガタ
唐銕紋
タウテツモン
古銅紋
コドウモン
唐紋
カラモン
鳳珠紋
ホウジユモン

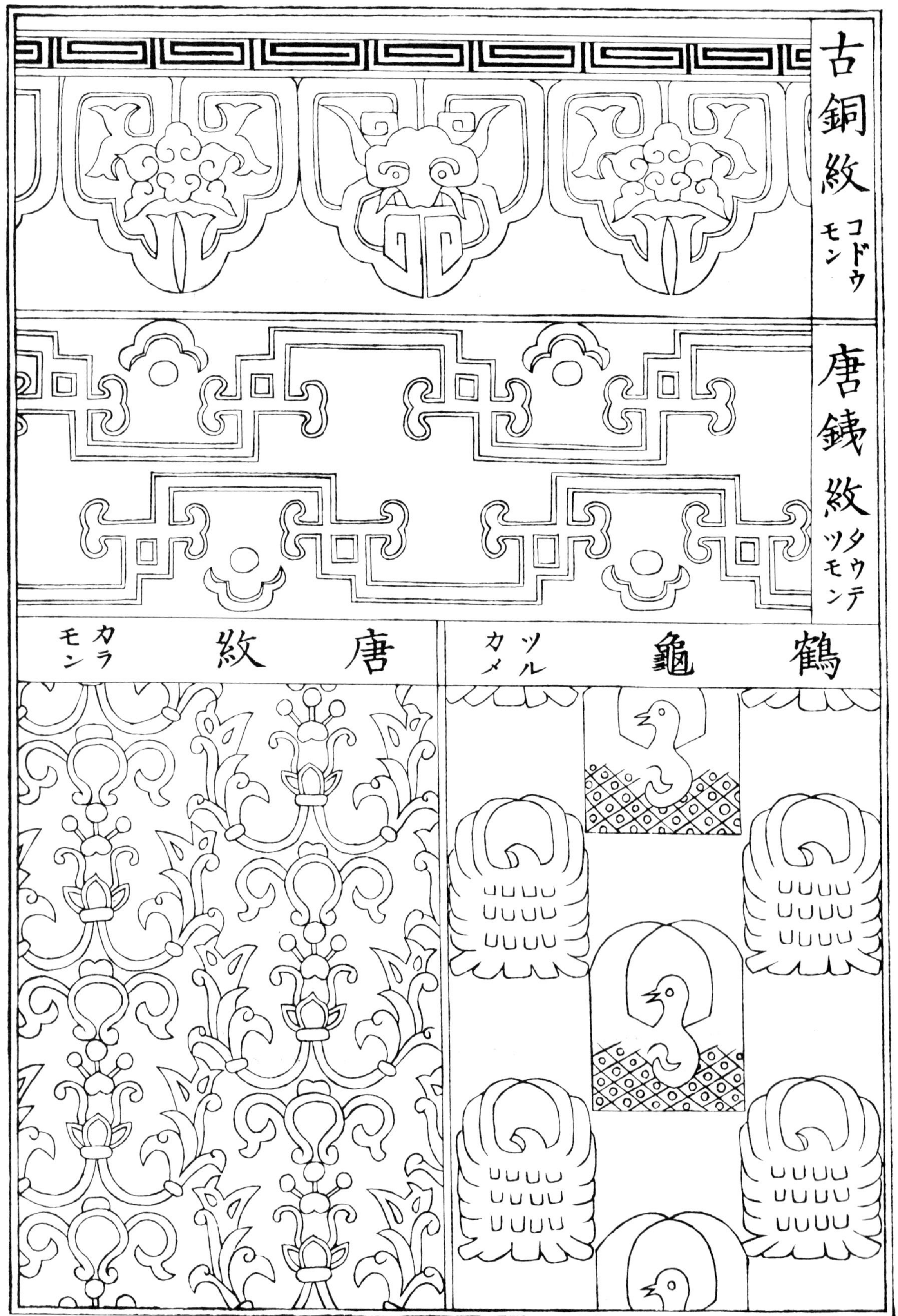
古銅紋
コドウモン
唐銭紋
タウテツモン
鶴亀
ツルカメ
唐紋
カラモン

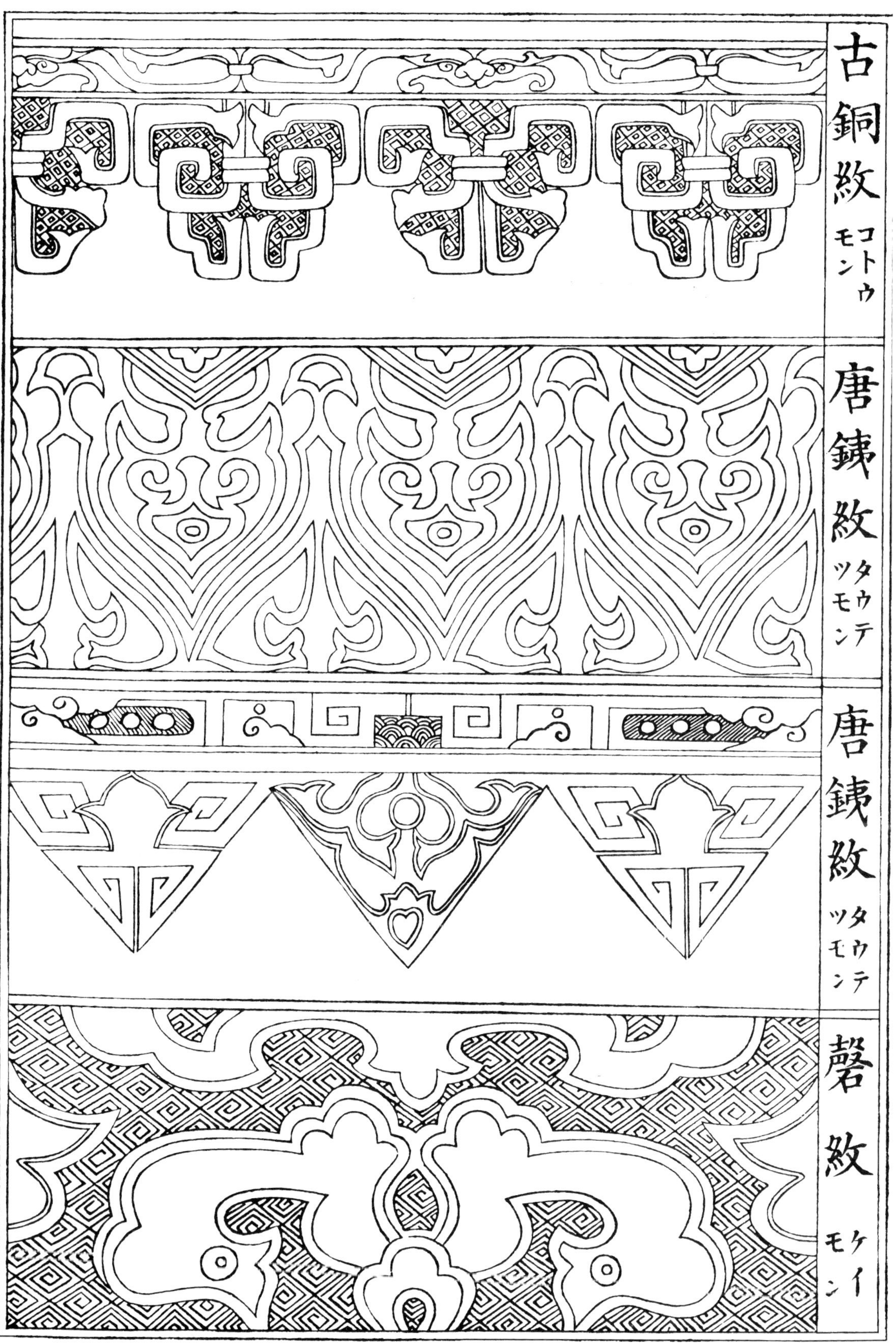
古銅紋
コトウモン
唐銕紋
タウテツモン
唐銕紋
タウテツモン
磬紋
ケイモン

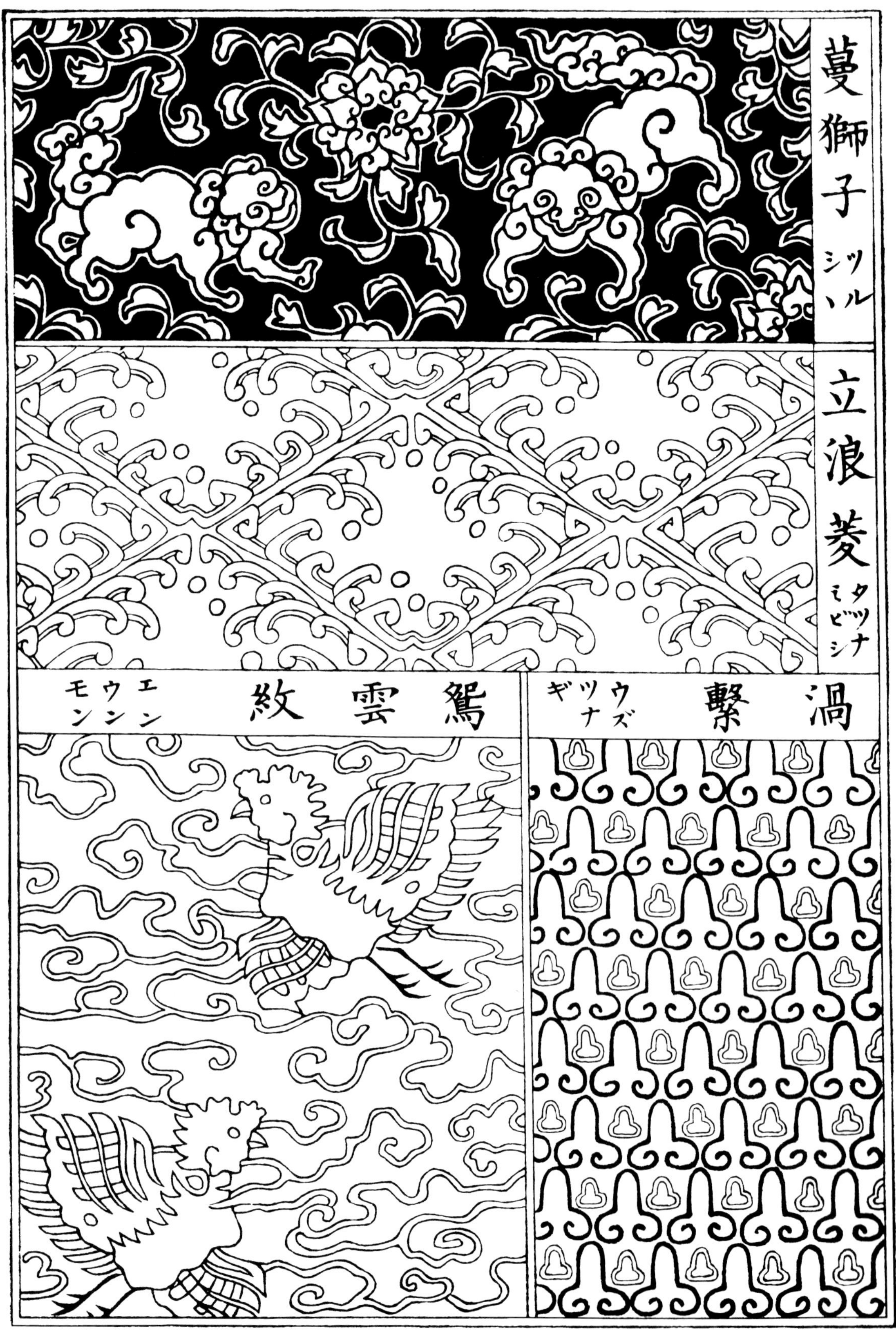

蔓獅子
ツルシヽ
立浪菱
タツナミビシ
鴛雲紋
エンウンモン
渦繋
ウズツナギ

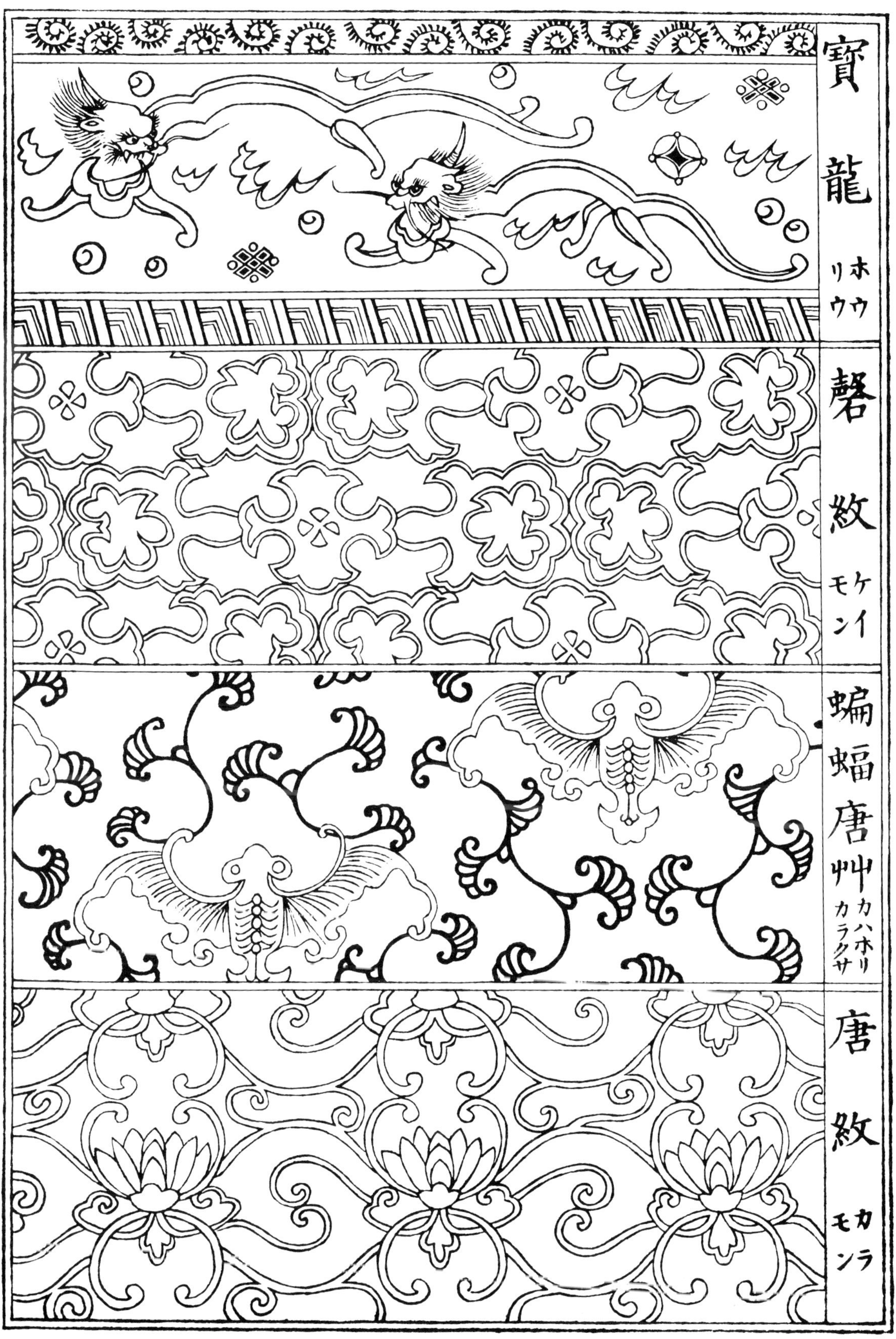
寶龍 ホウリウ
磬紋 ケイモン
蝙蝠唐艸 カハホリカラクサ
唐紋 カラモン

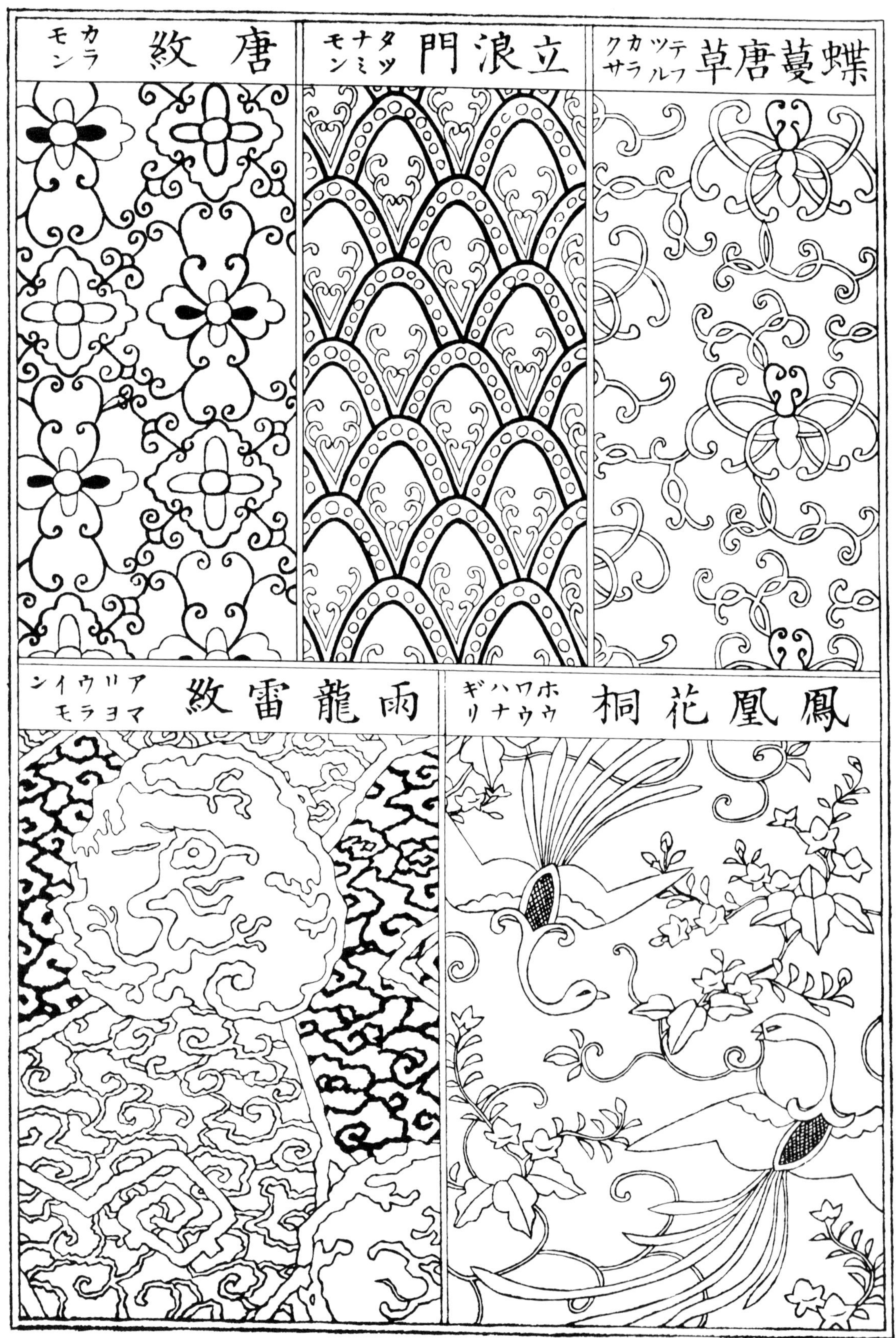

唐紋 カラモン
立浪門 タツナミモン
蝶蔓唐草 テフツルカラクサ
雨龍雷紋 アマリヨウライモン
鳳凰花桐 ホウワウハナギリ

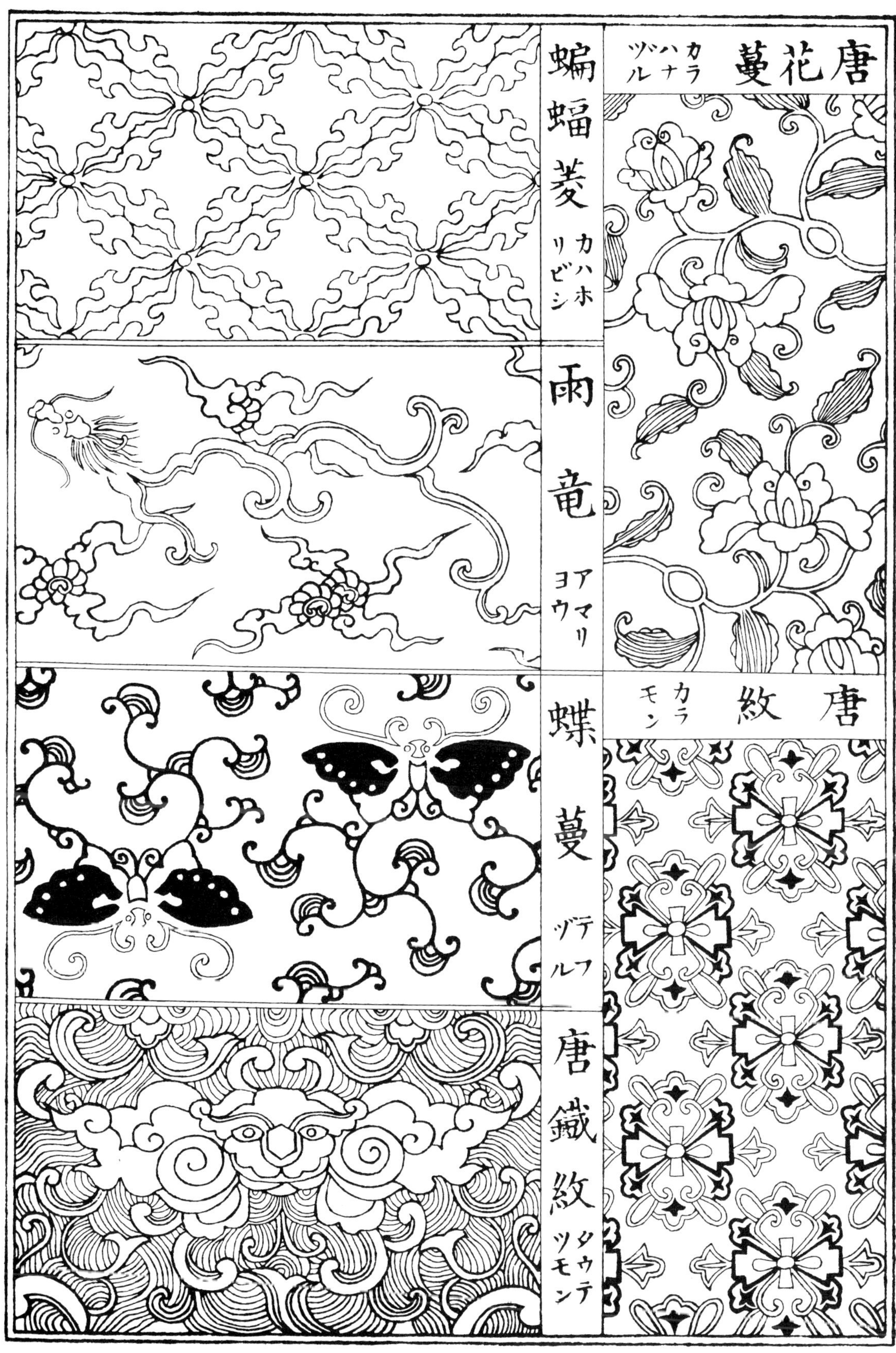
唐花蔓 カラハナヅル
蝙蝠菱 カハホリビシ
雨竜 アマリヨウ
唐紋 カラモン
蝶蔓 テフヅル
唐鐵紋 タウテツモン

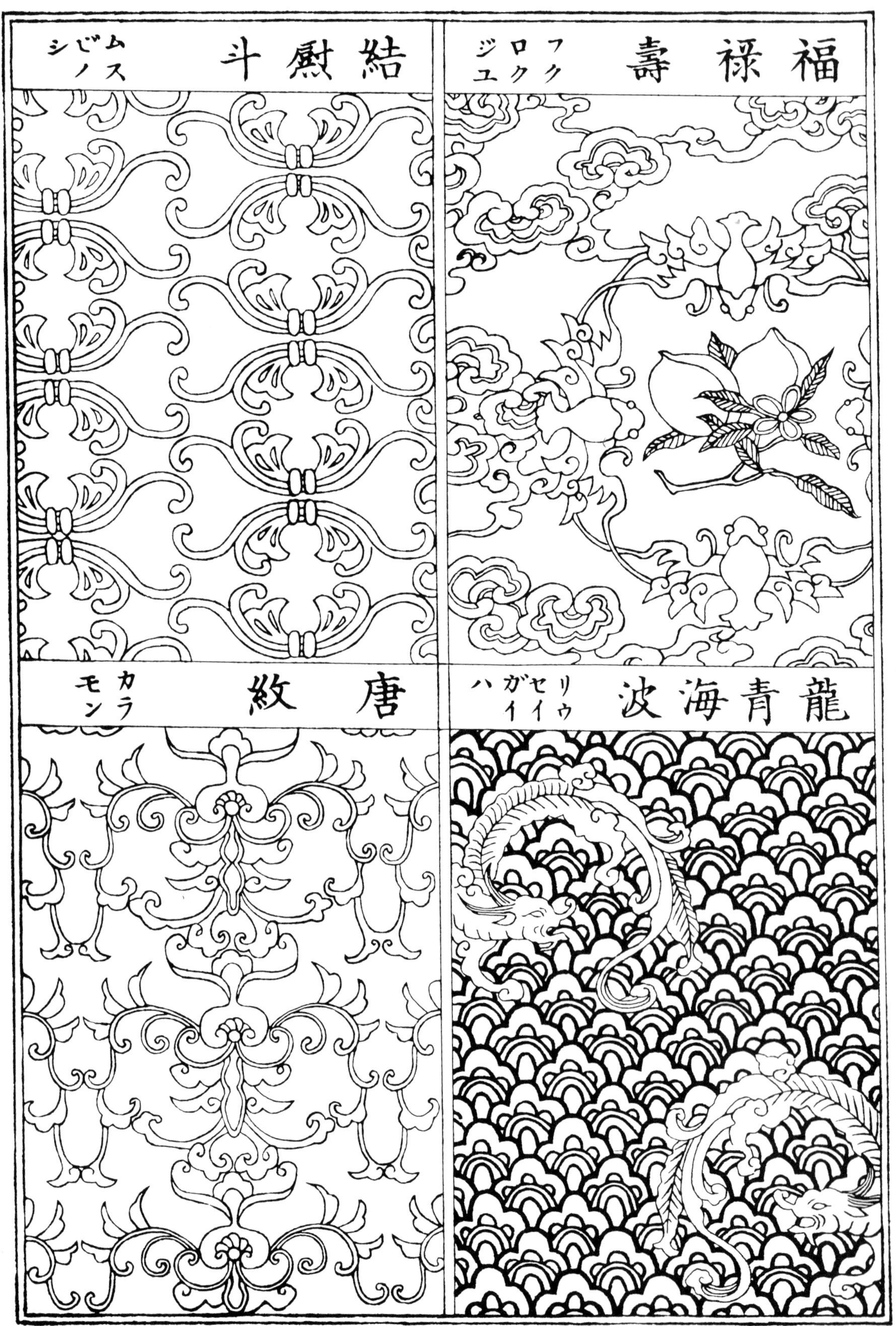

結熨斗 ムスビノシ
福祿壽 フクロクジユ
唐紋 カラモン
龍青海波 リウセイガイハ

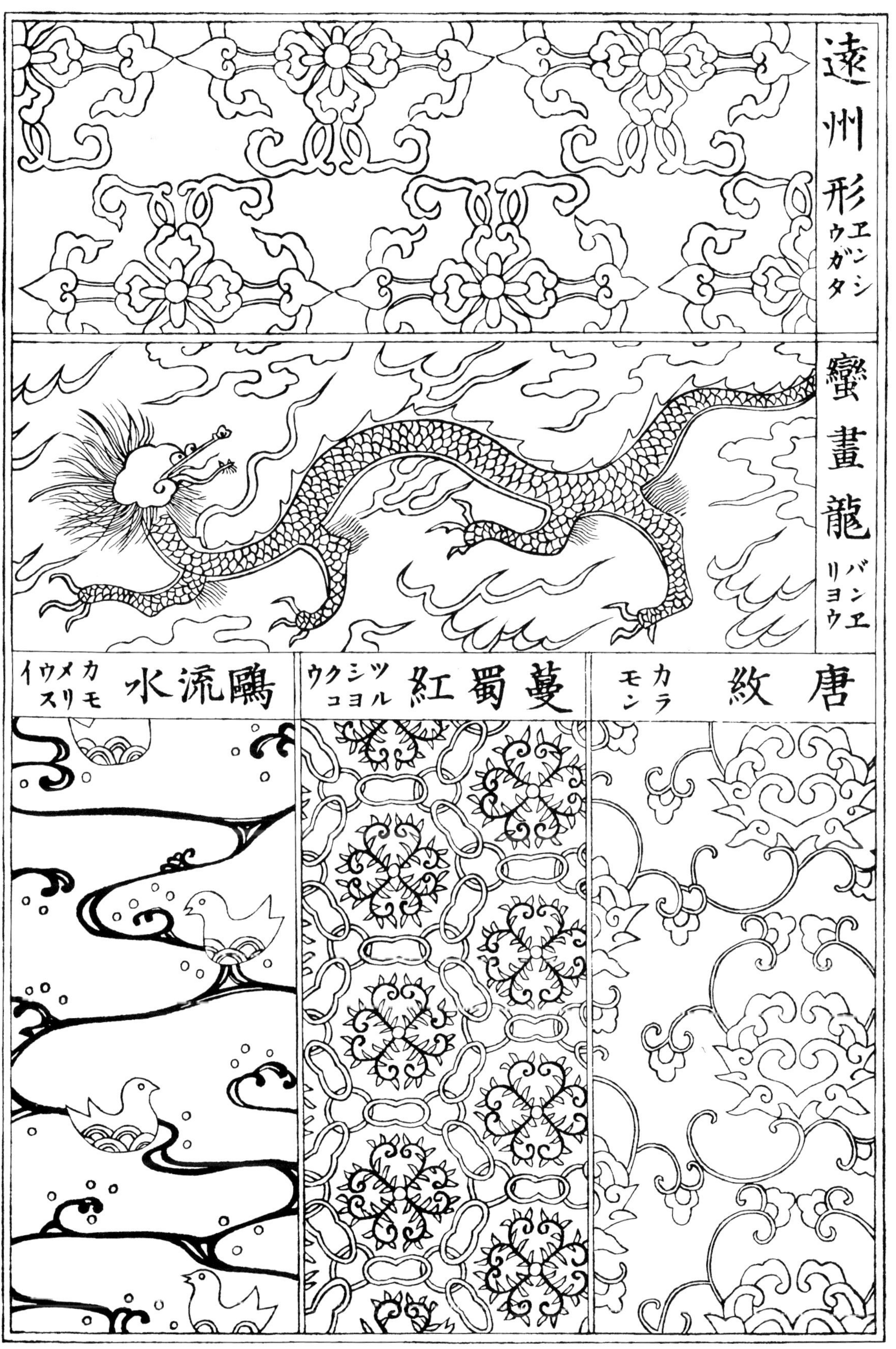
遠州形 エンシウガタ
蠻畫龍 バンヱリヨウ
唐紋 カラモン
蔓蜀紅 ツルシヨクコウ
鷗流水 カモメリウスイ

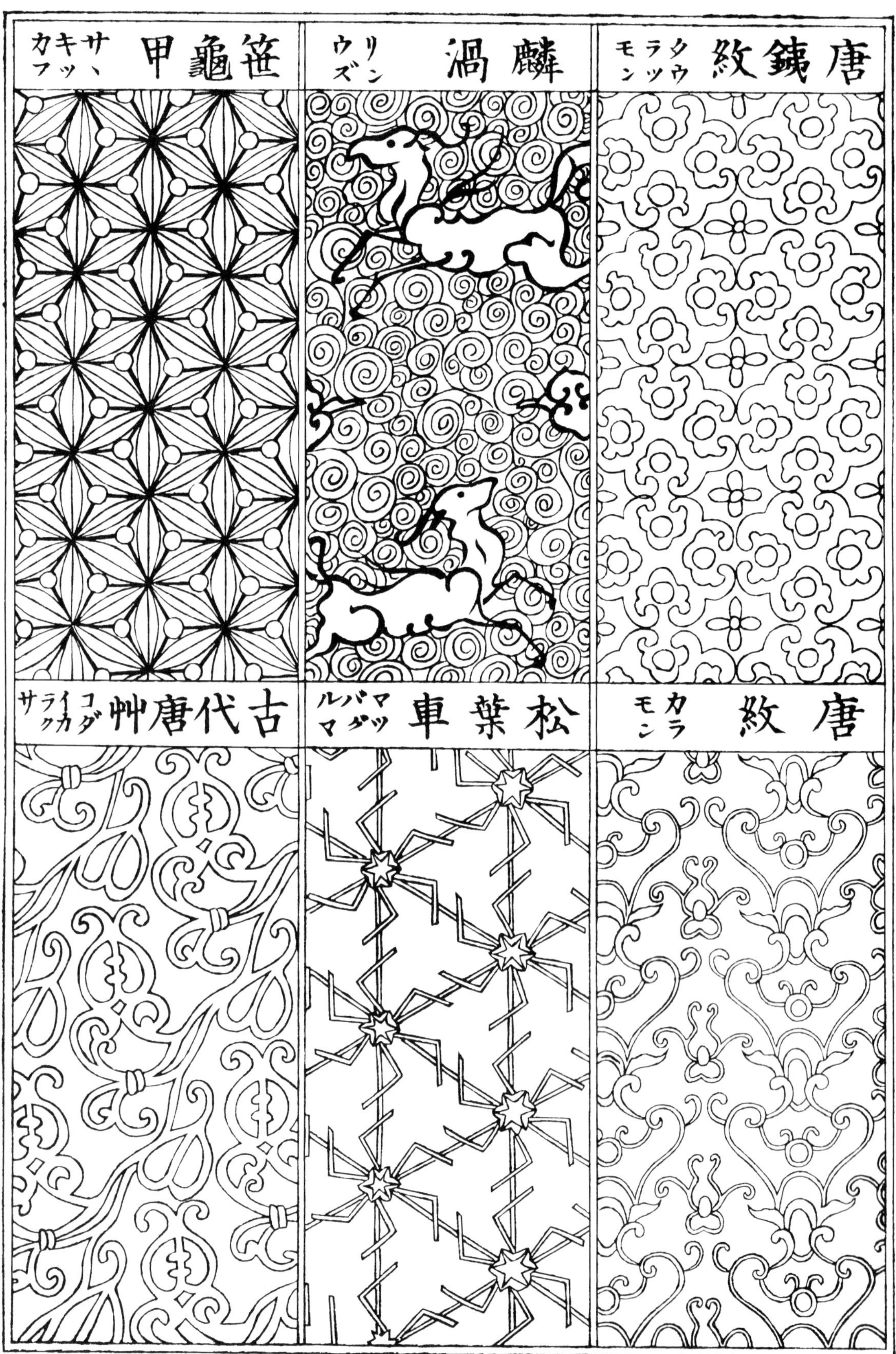

笹亀甲
麟渦
唐錢紋
古代唐艸
松葉車
唐紋

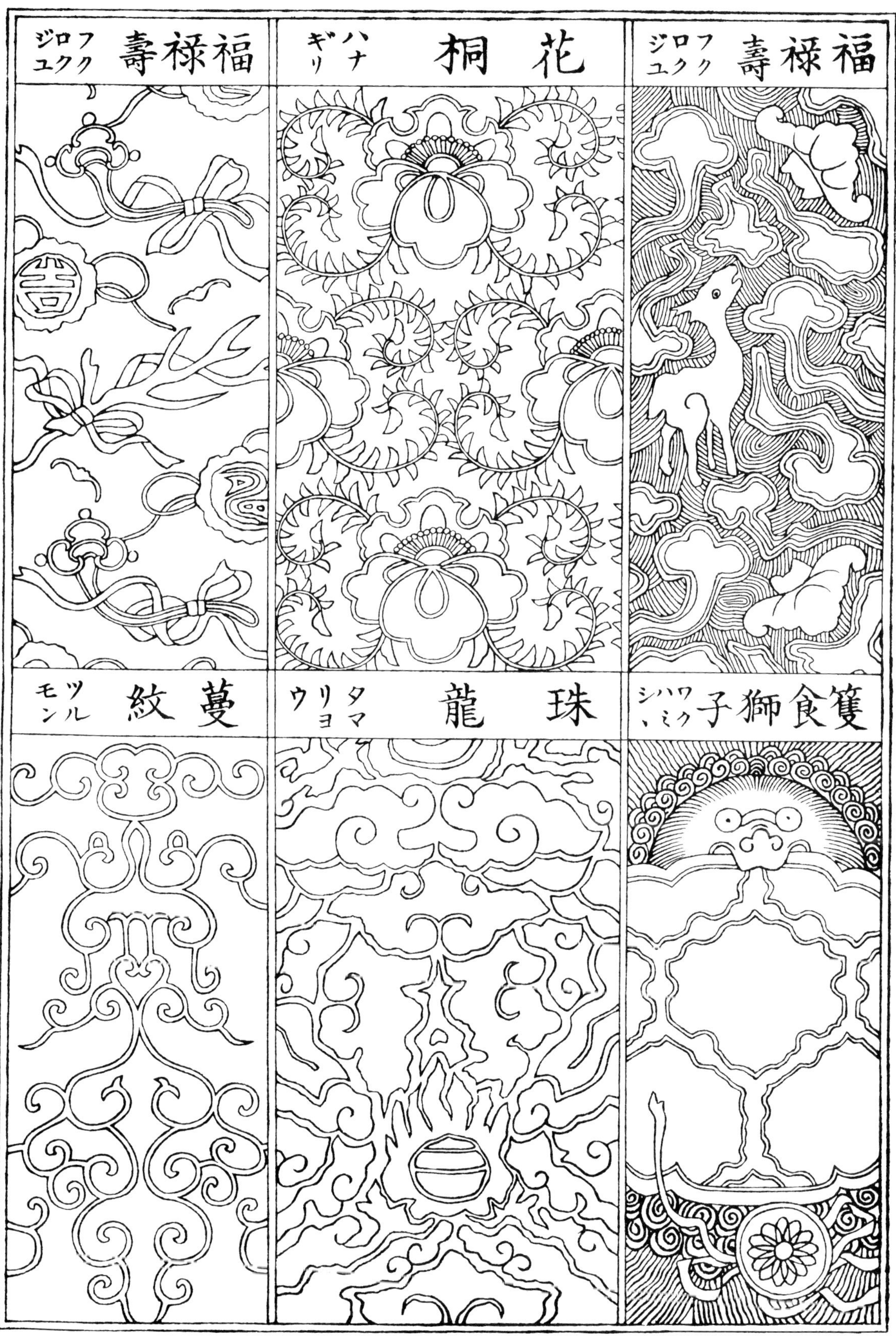
福祿壽 フクロクジユ
花桐 ハナギリ
福祿壽 フクロクジユ
蔓紋 ツルモン
珠龍 タマリヨウ
篗食獅子 ワクハミシヽ

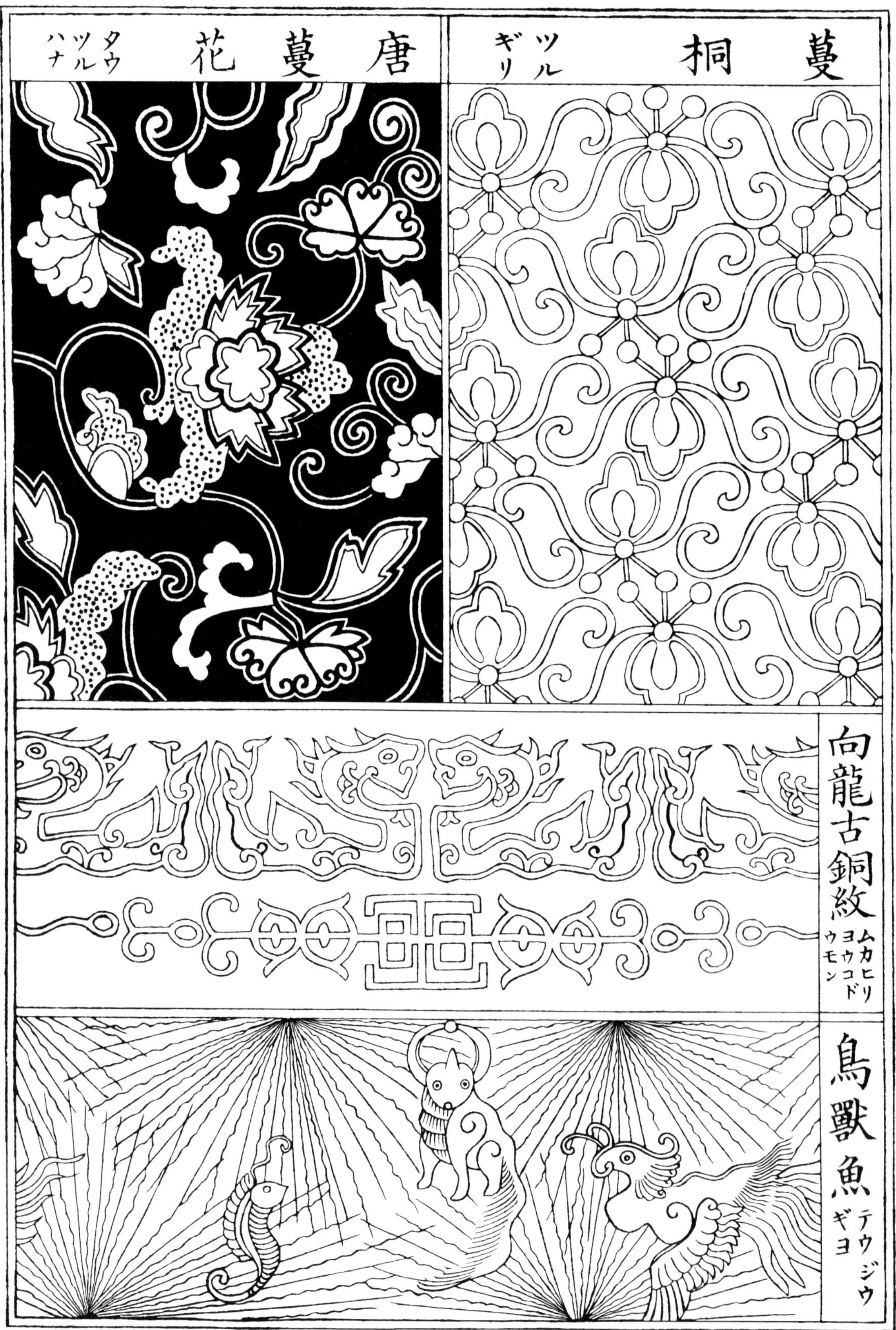
唐蔓花 タウツルハナ
蔓桐 ツルギリ
向龍古銅紋 ムカヒリヨウコドウモン
鳥獸魚 テウジウギヨ

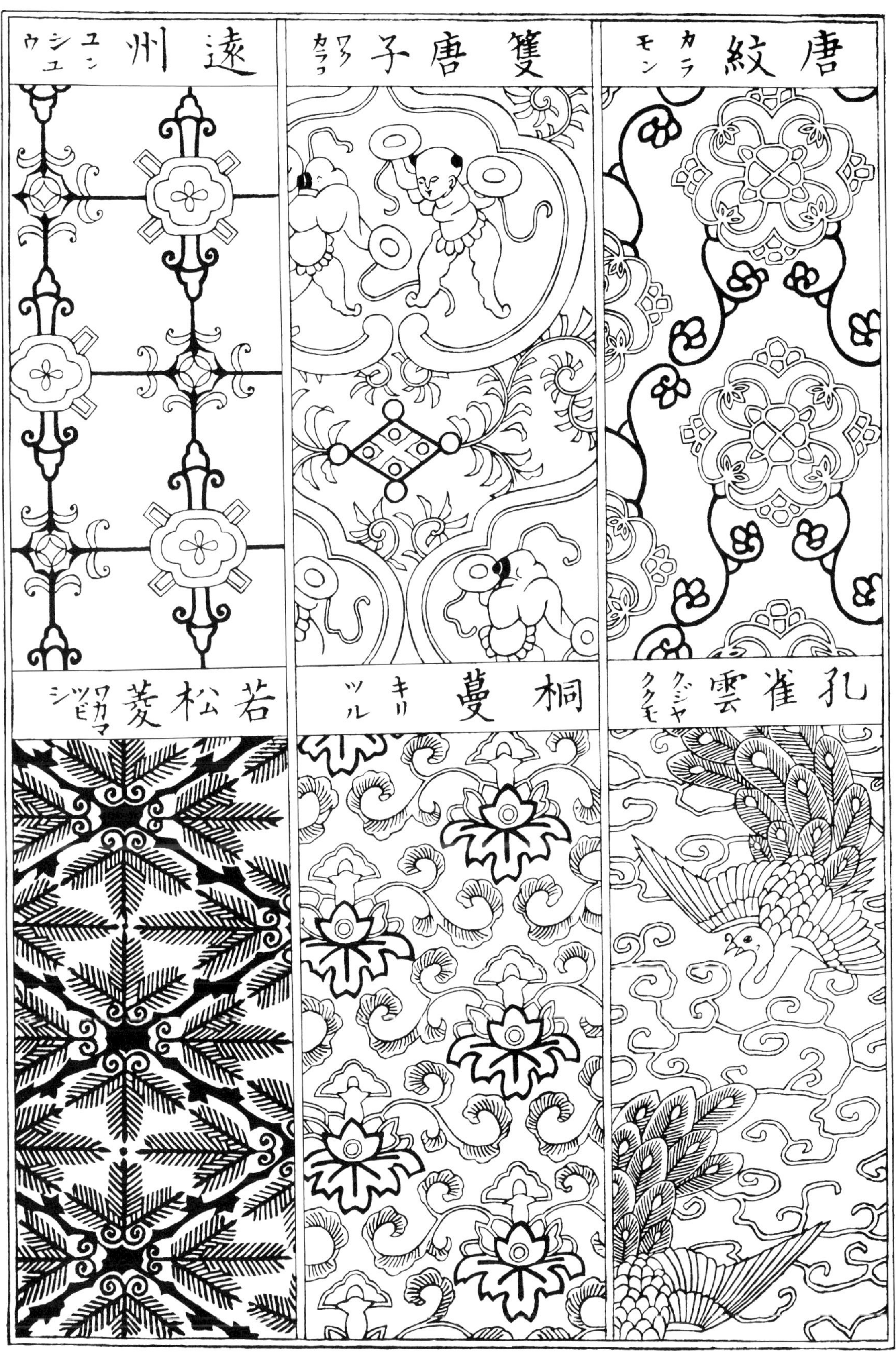
遠州 エンシュウ
籰唐子 ワクカラコ
唐紋 カラモン
若松菱 ワカマツビシ
桐蔓 キリツル
孔雀雲 クジャククモ

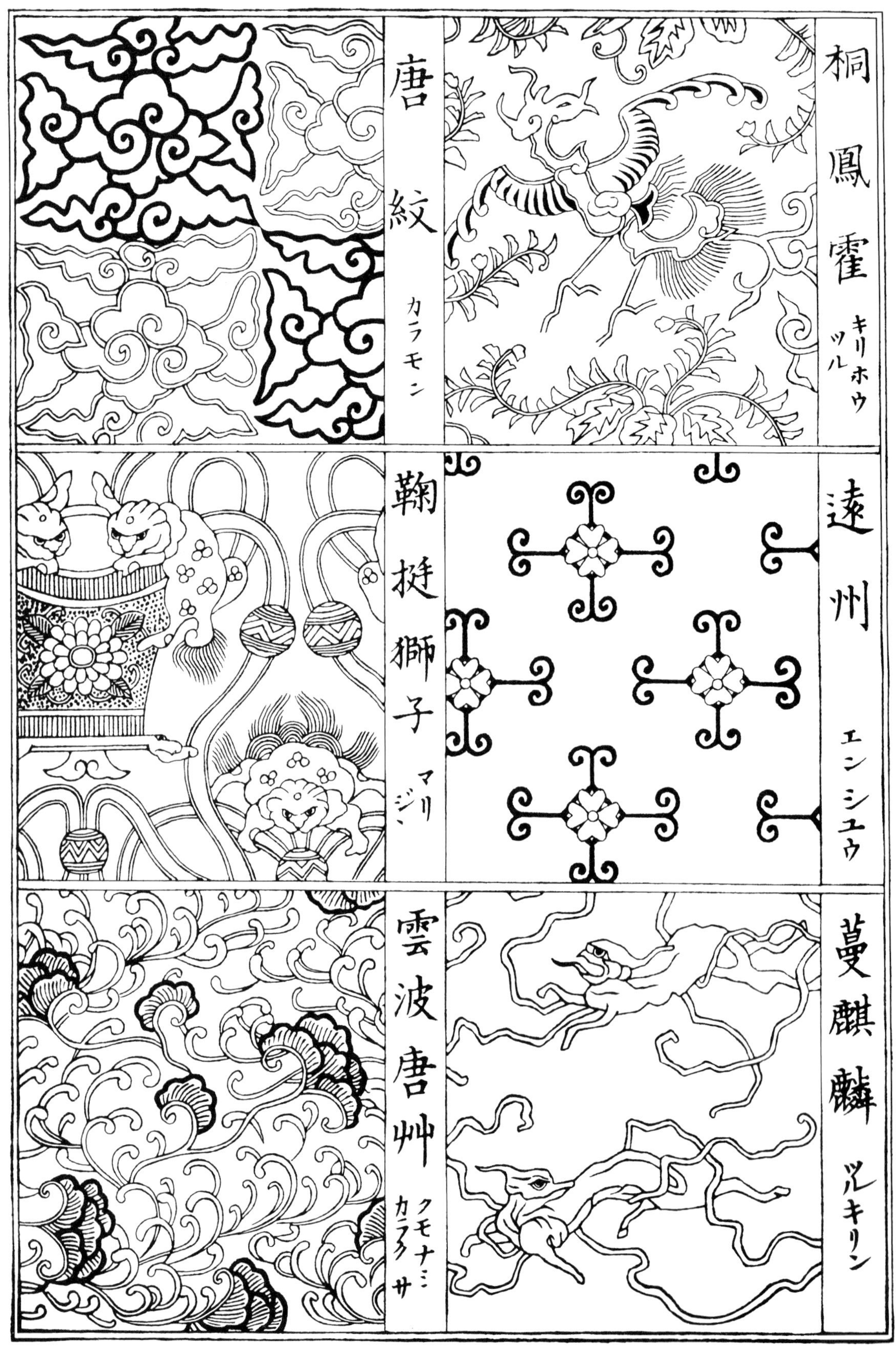
桐鳳霍
キリホウツル
唐紋
カラモン
遠州
エンシユウ
鞠挺獅子
マリジヽ
蔓麒麟
ツルキリン
雲波唐艸
クモナミカラクサ

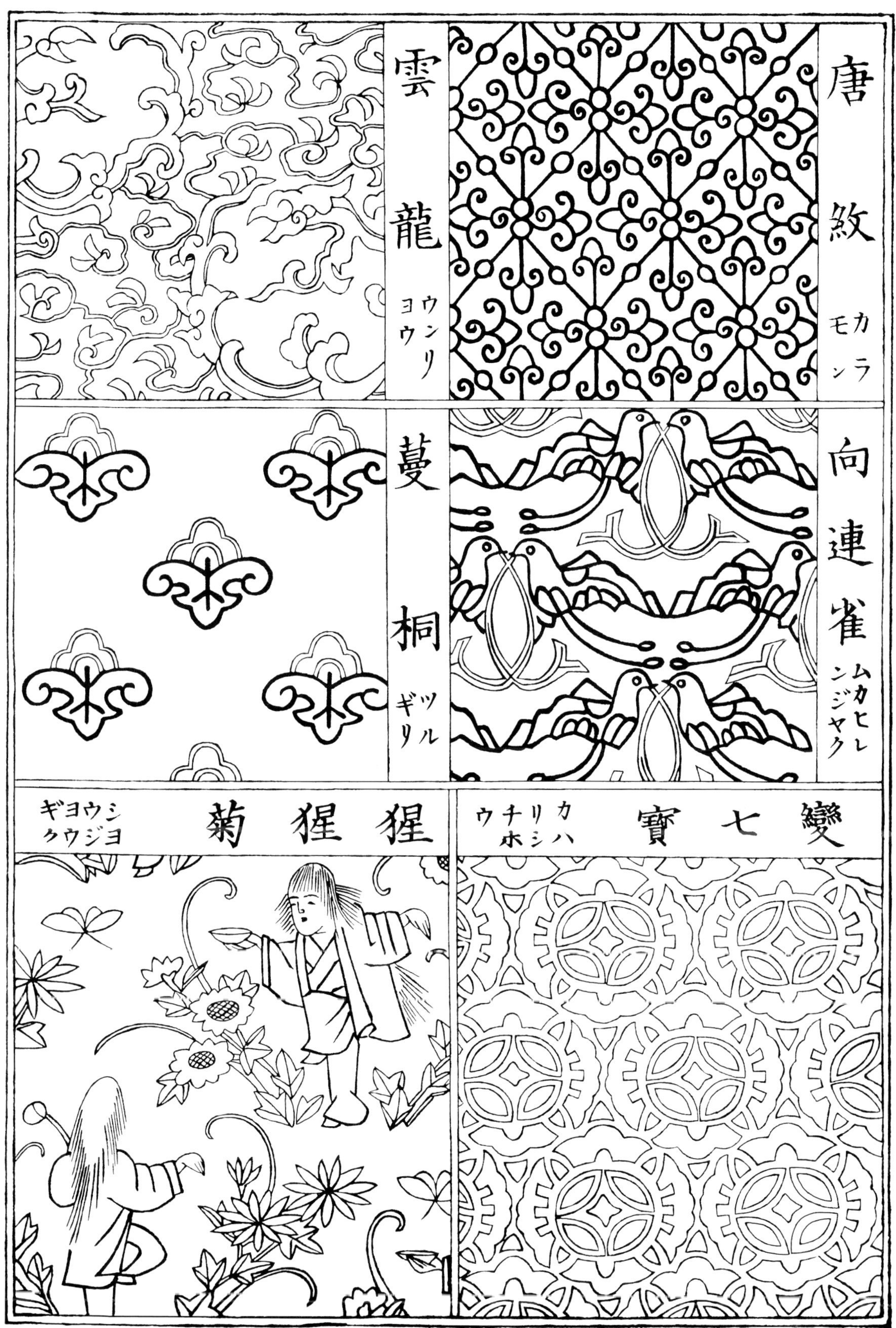

唐紋
カラモン
雲龍
ウンリヨウ
向連雀
ムカヒレンジヤク
蔓桐
ツルギリ
變七寶
カハリシチホウ
猩猩菊
シヨウジヨウギク

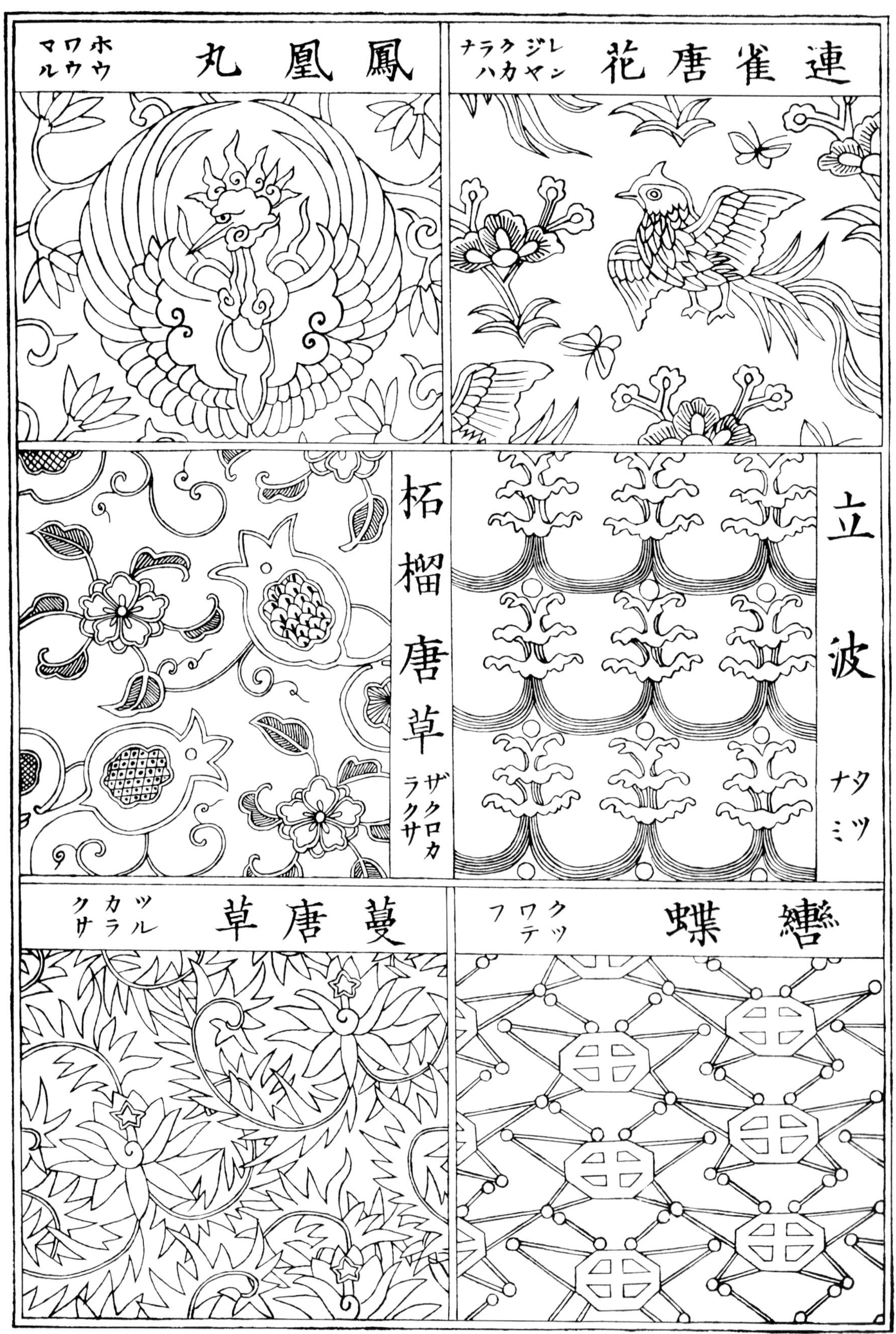
鳳凰丸 ホウワウマル
連雀唐花 レンジヤクカラハナ
柘榴唐草 ザクロカラクサ
立波 タツナミ
蔓唐草 ツルカラクサ
轡蝶 クツワテフ

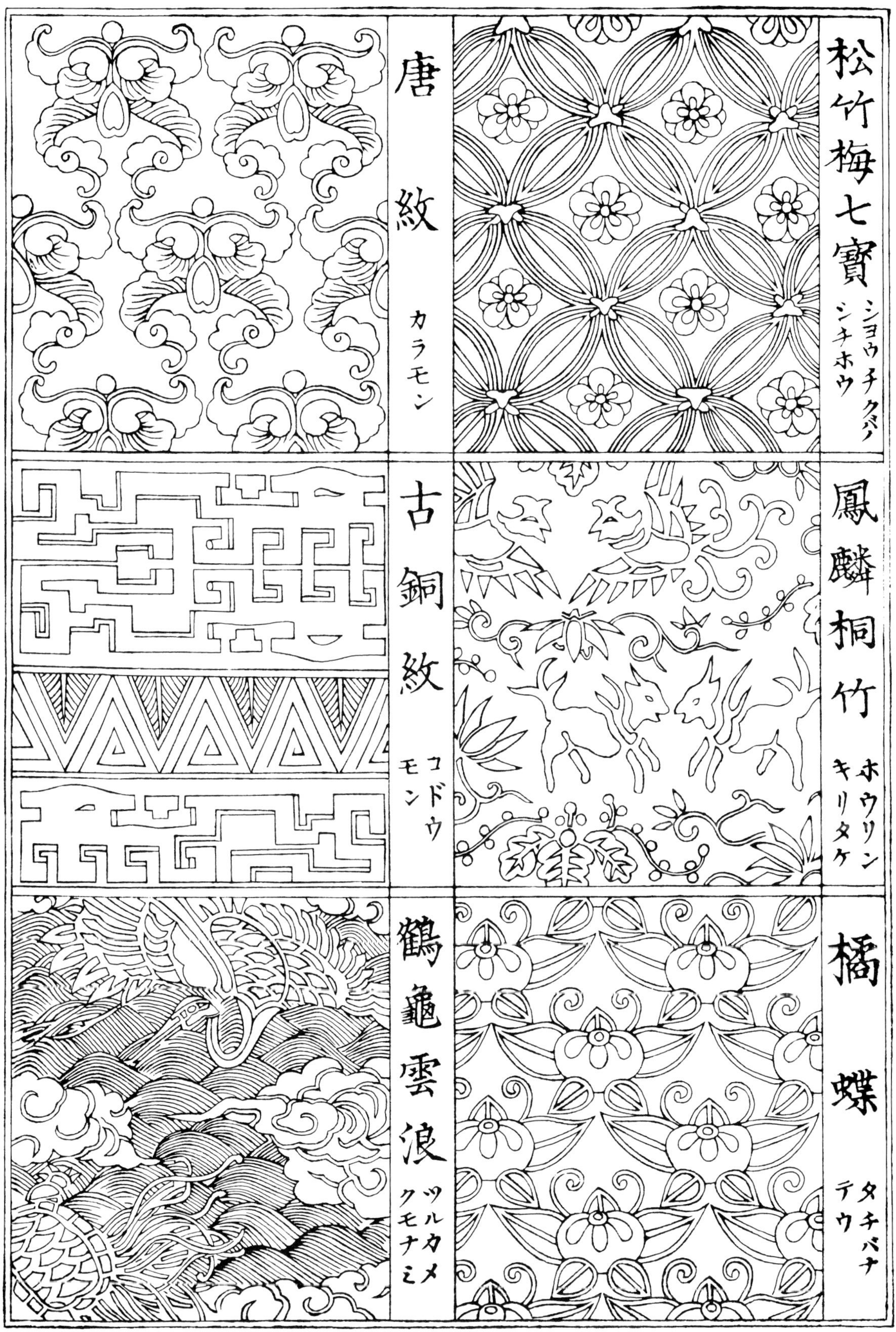
松竹梅七寶
シヨウチクバノ
シチホウ
唐紋
カラモン
鳳麟桐竹
ホウリン
キリタケ
古銅紋
コドウ
モン
橘蝶
タチバナ
テウ
鶴亀雲浪
ツルカメ
クモナミ

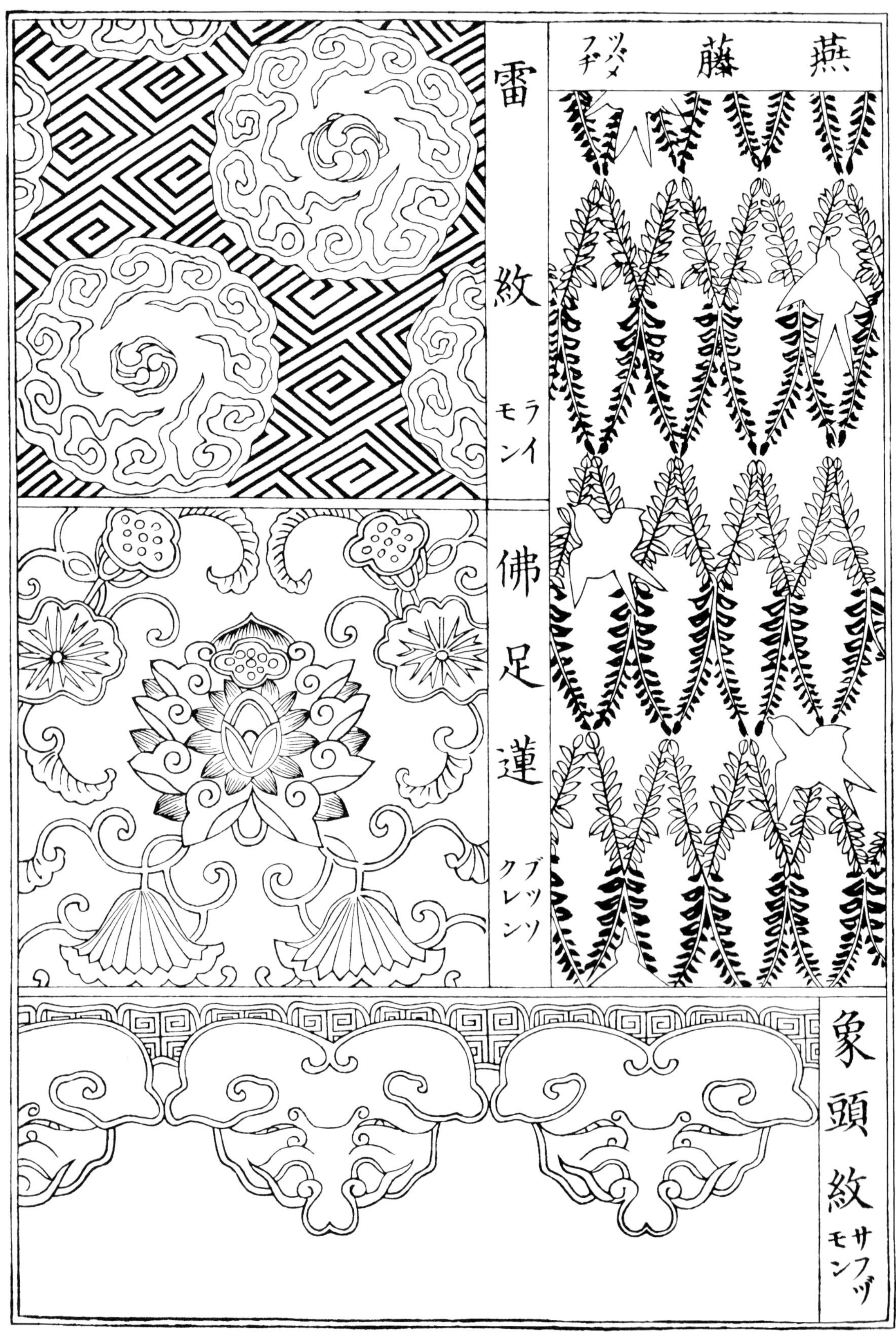

雷紋
ライモン
燕藤
ツバメフヂ
佛足蓮
ブッソクレン
象頭紋
サフヅモン

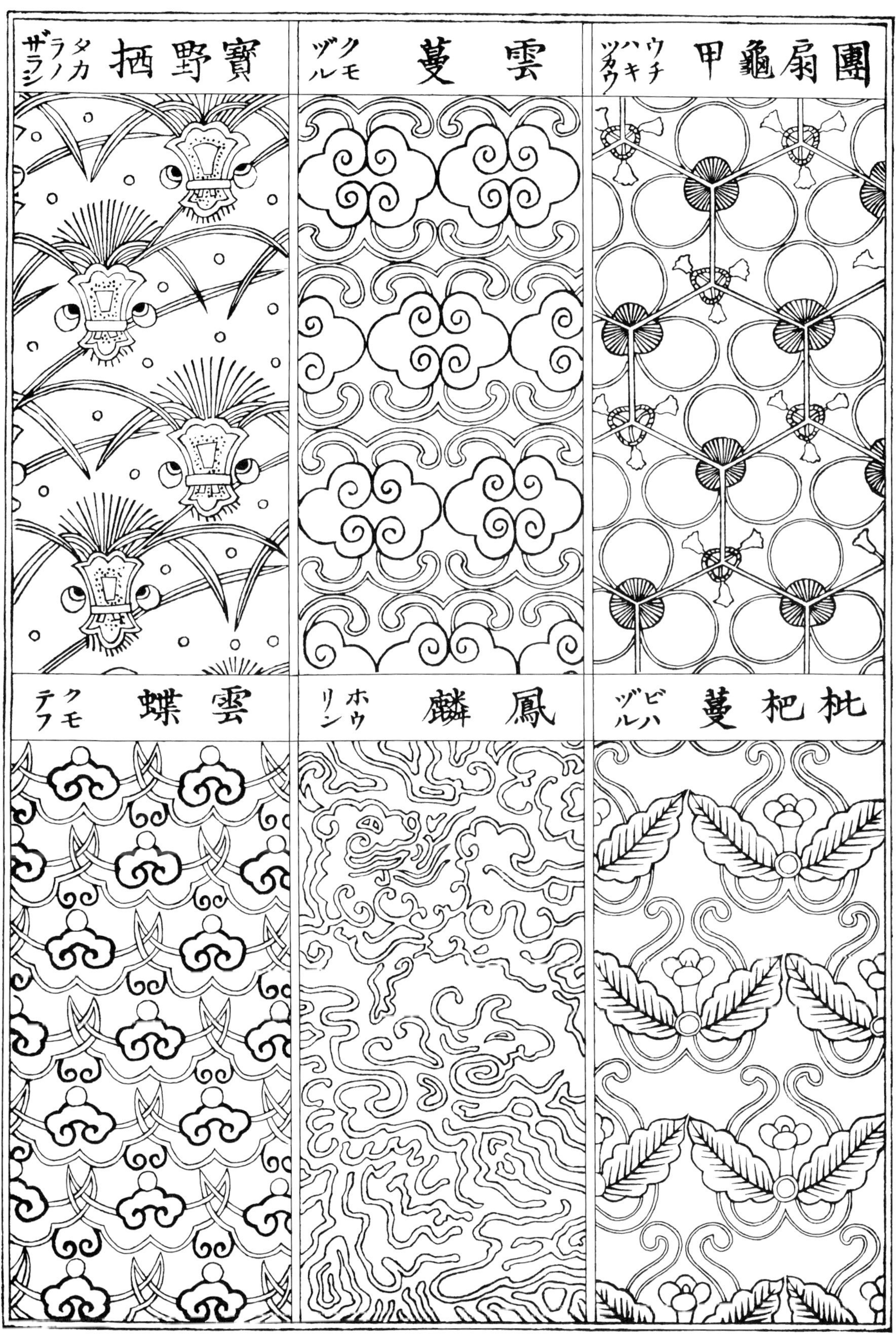

寶野栖
タカラノザラシ
雲蔓
クモヅル
團扇龜甲
ウチハキツカウ
雲蝶
クモテフ
鳳麟
ホウリン
枇杷蔓
ビハヅル

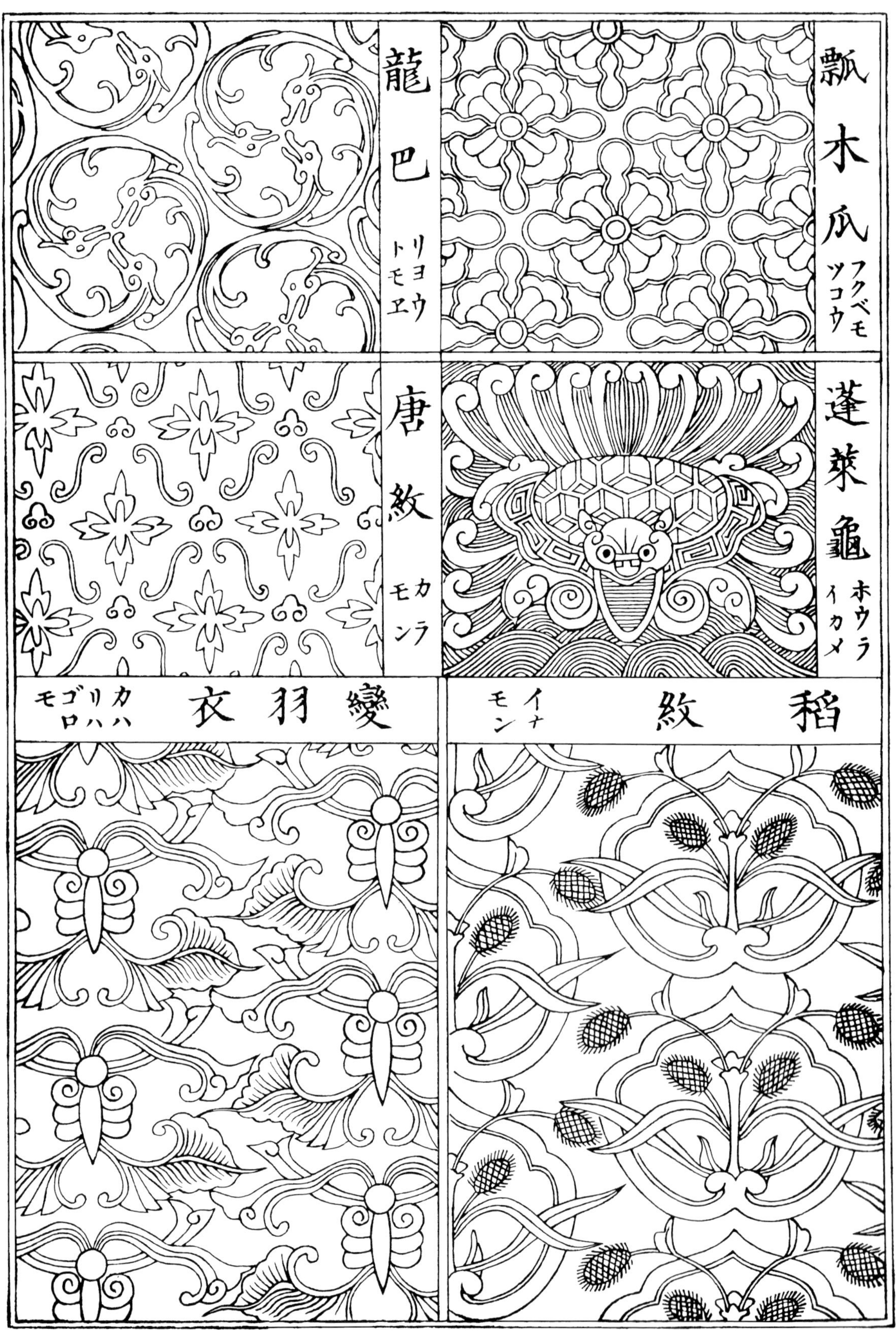
瓢木瓜
フクベモツコウ
龍巴
リヨウトモヱ
蓬莱亀
ホウライカメ
唐紋
カラモン
稻紋
イナモン
變羽衣
カハリハゴロモ

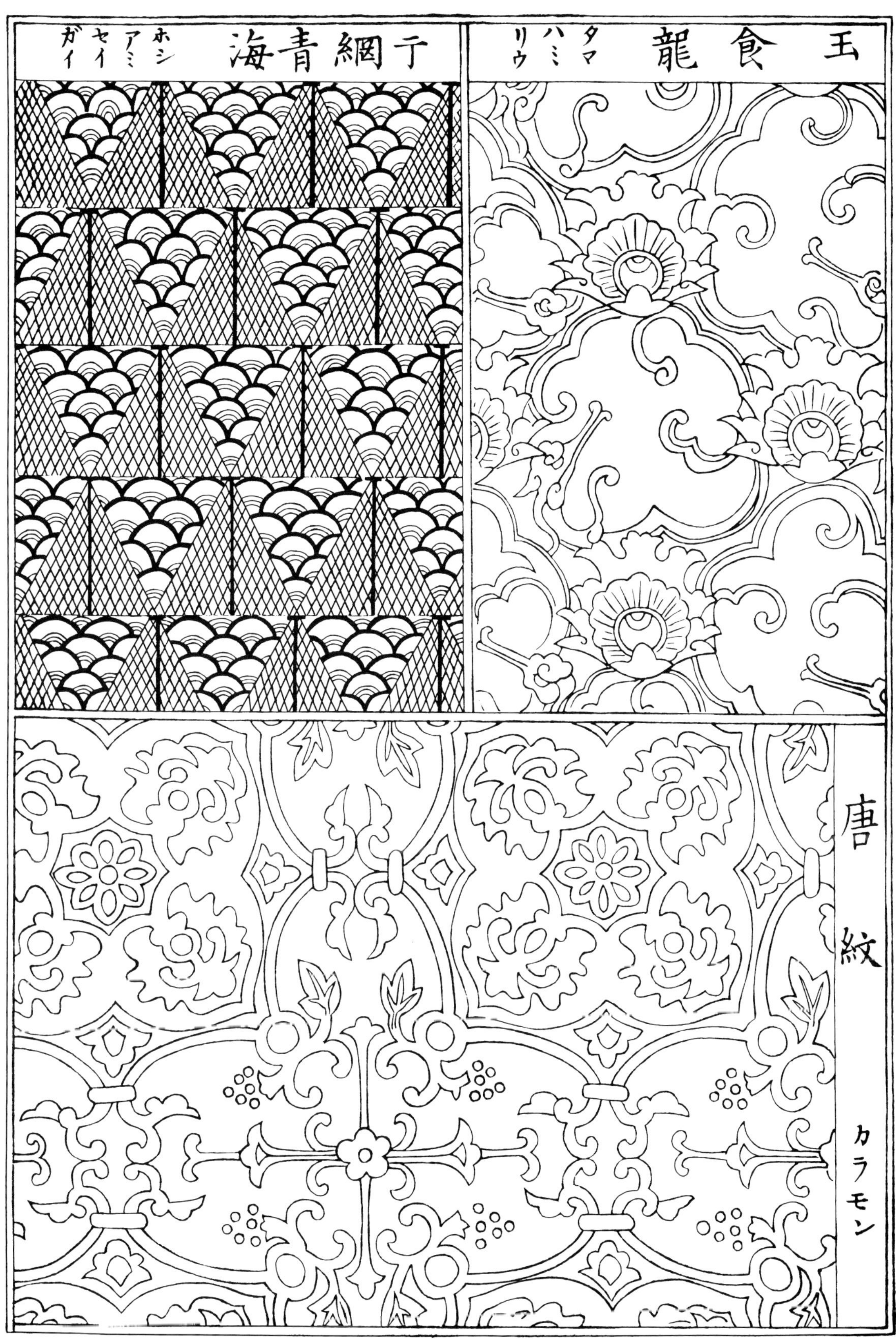
丁綱青海
ホシアミセイガイ
玉食龍
タマハミリウ
唐紋
カラモン

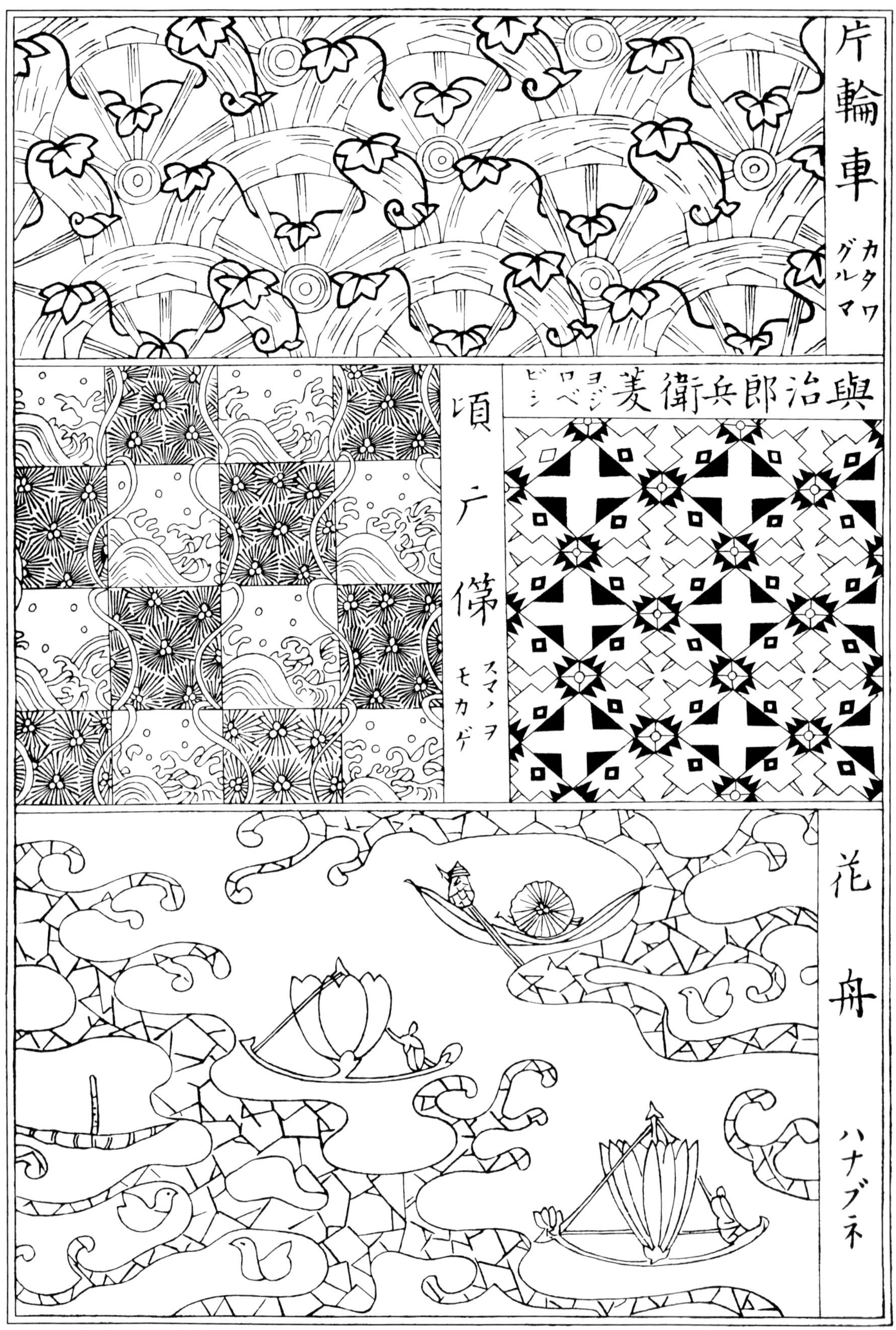
片輪車
カタワグルマ
與治郎兵衛菱
ヨジロベビシ
頃广俤
スマノヲモカゲ
花舟
ハナブネ

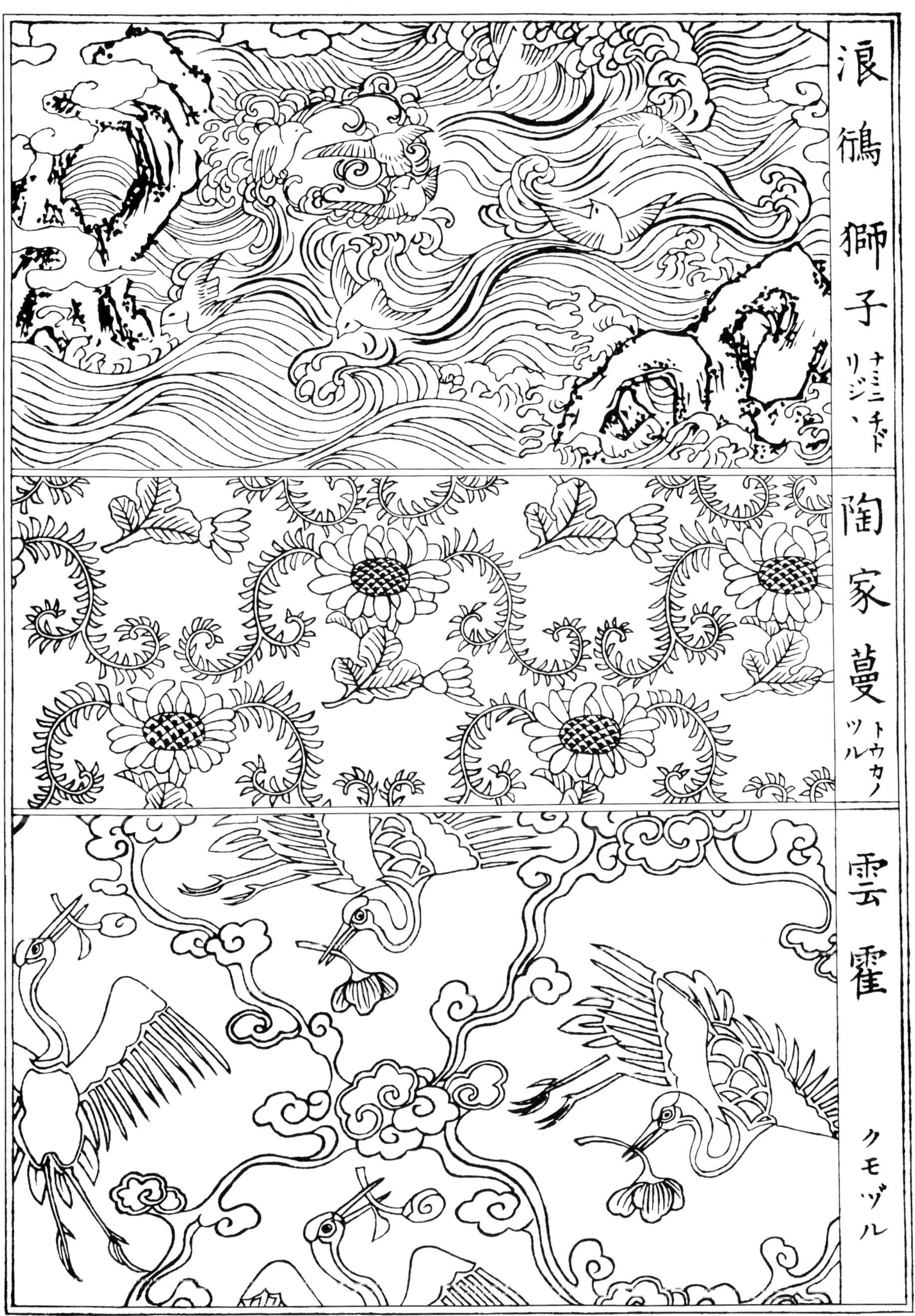
浪鵆獅子
ナミニチドリジヽ
陶家蔓
トウカノツル
雲霍
クモヅル

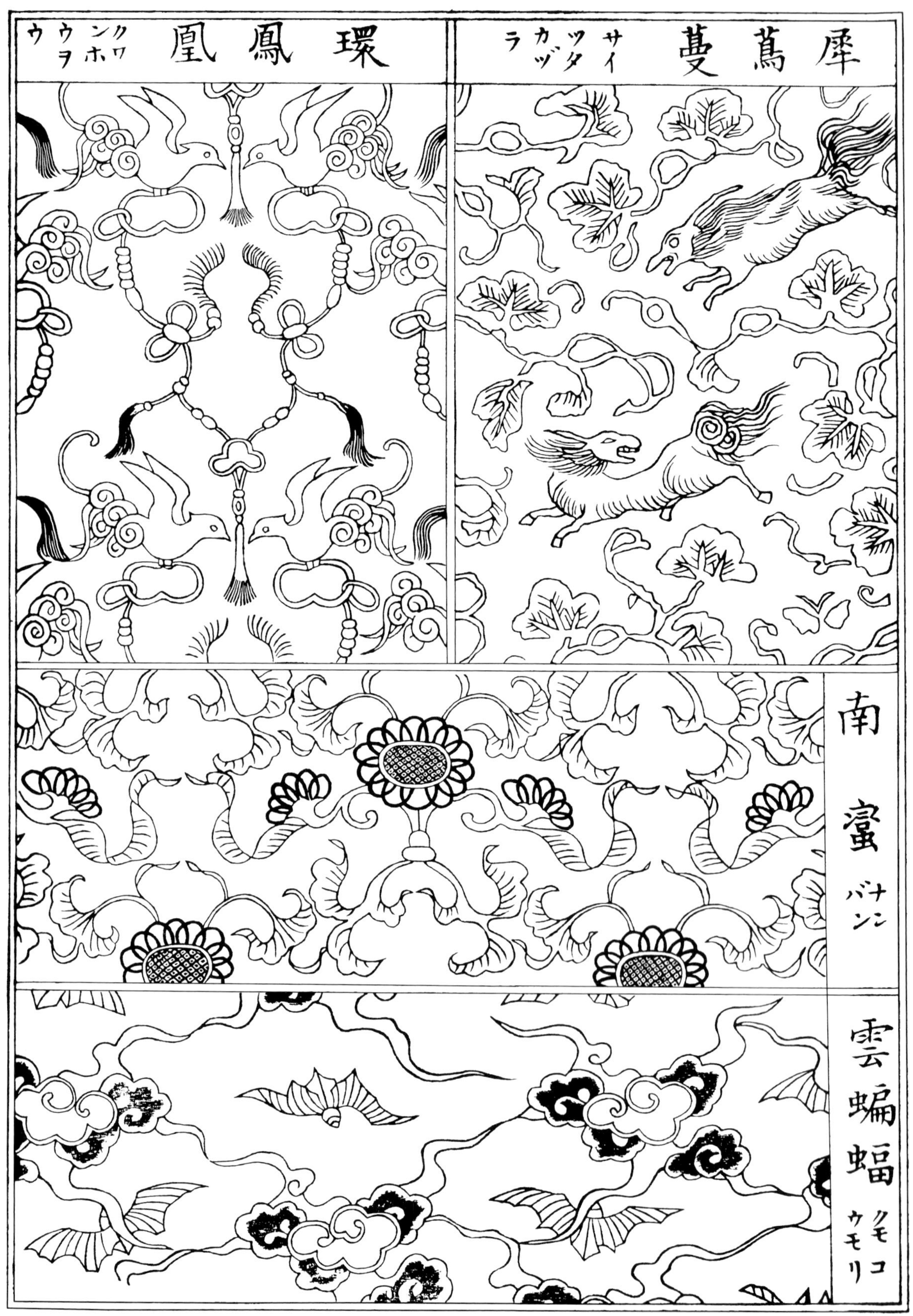

環鳳凰
クワンホウヲウ
犀蔦蔓
サイツタカヅラ
南蛮
ナンバン
雲蝙蝠
クモコウモリ

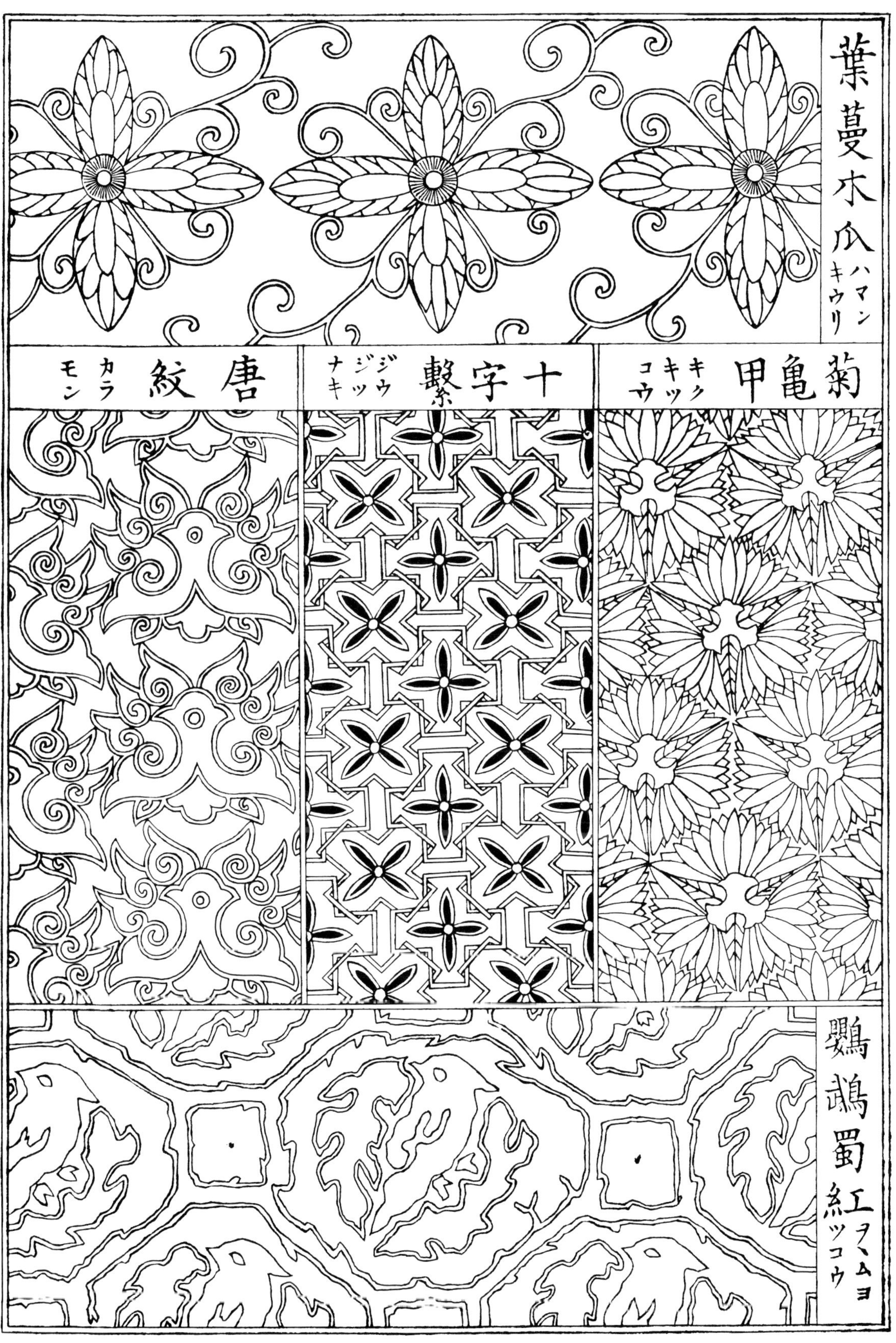

葉蔓木瓜 ハマンキウリ
菊亀甲 キクキツコウ
十字繫 ジウジツナキ
唐紋 カラモン
鸚鵡蜀紅 ヲヽムヨツコウ

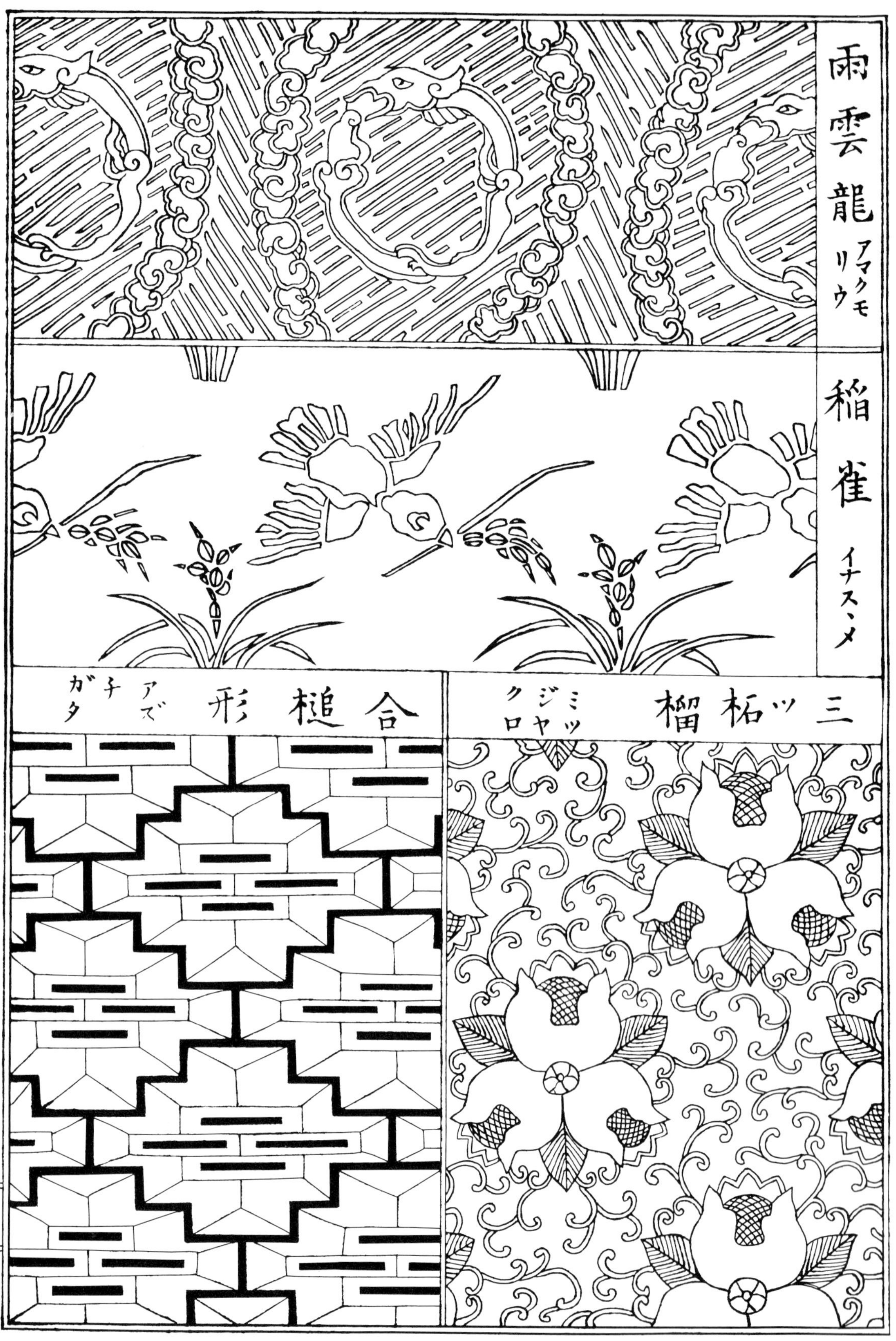

雨雲龍
アマクモリウ
稲雀
イナスゝメ
合槌形
アヅチガタ
三ッ柘榴
ミツジヤクロ

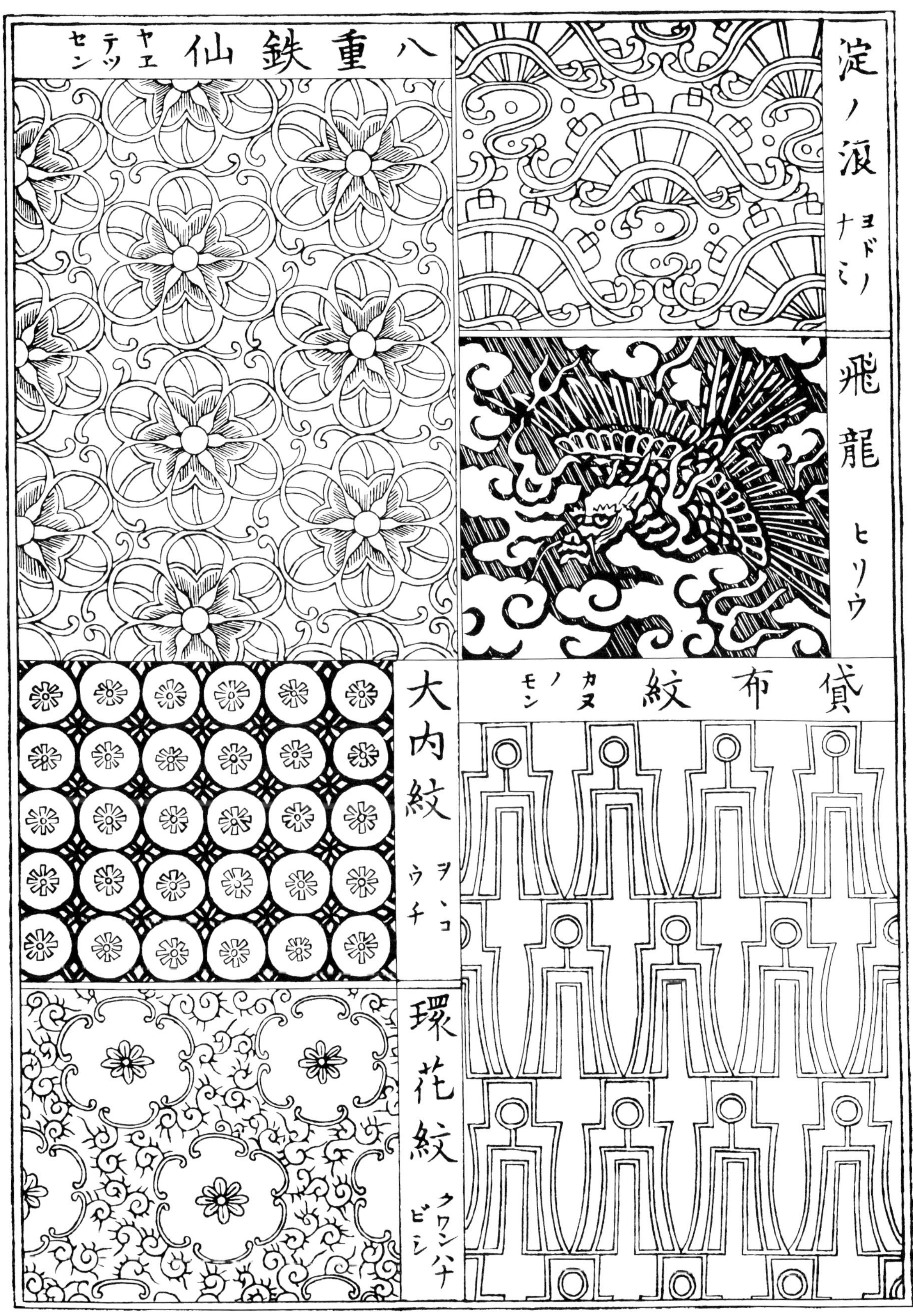
八重仙鉄
ヤヱセンテツ
淀ノ浪
ヨドノナミ
飛龍
ヒリウ
大内紋
オホウチモン
貨布紋
カヌノモン
環花紋
クワンハナビシ

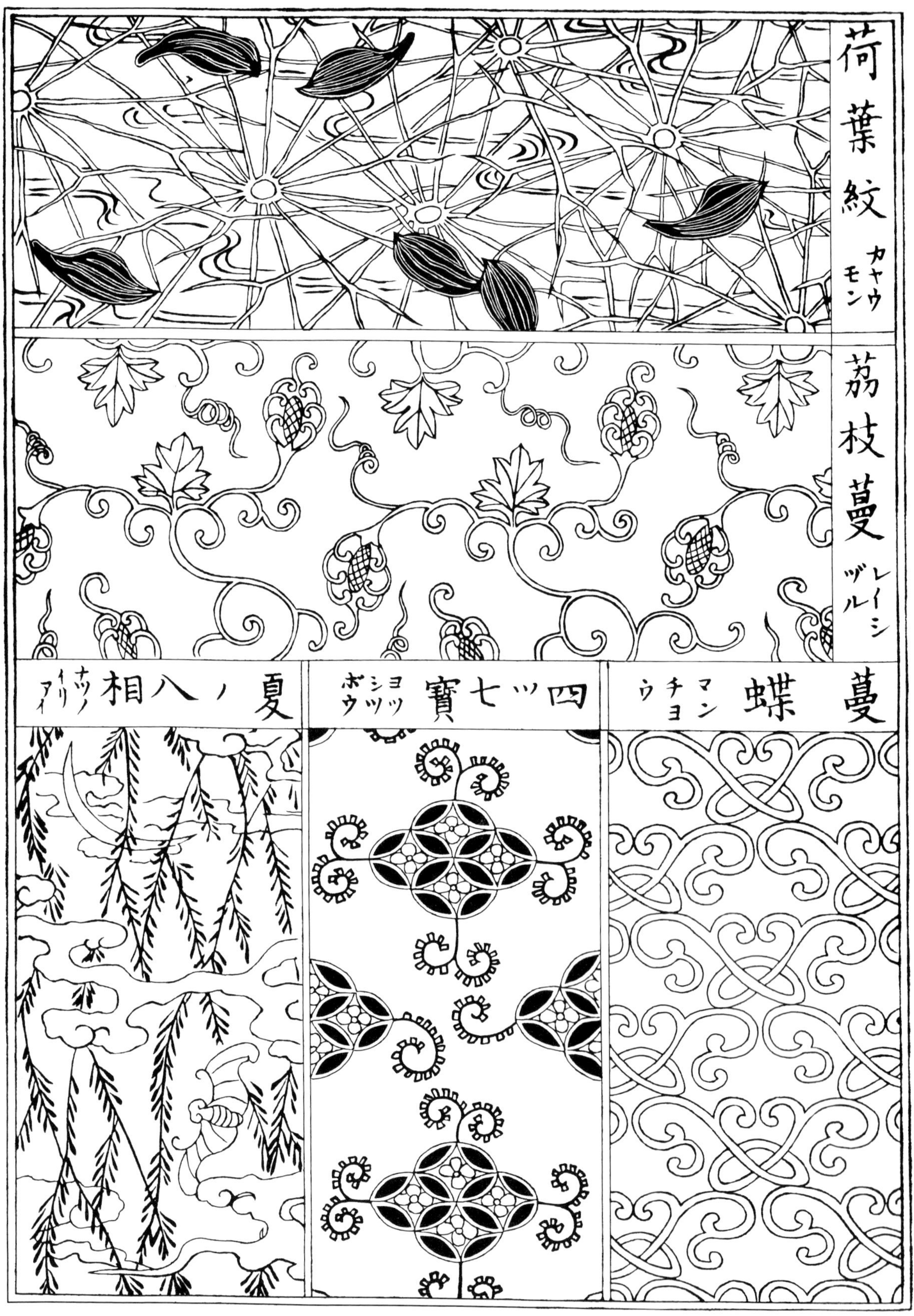
荷葉紋
カヤウモン
茘枝蔓
レイシヅル
夏ノ入相
ナツノイリアイ
四ツ七寶
ヨツシツポウ
蔓蝶
マンチヨウ

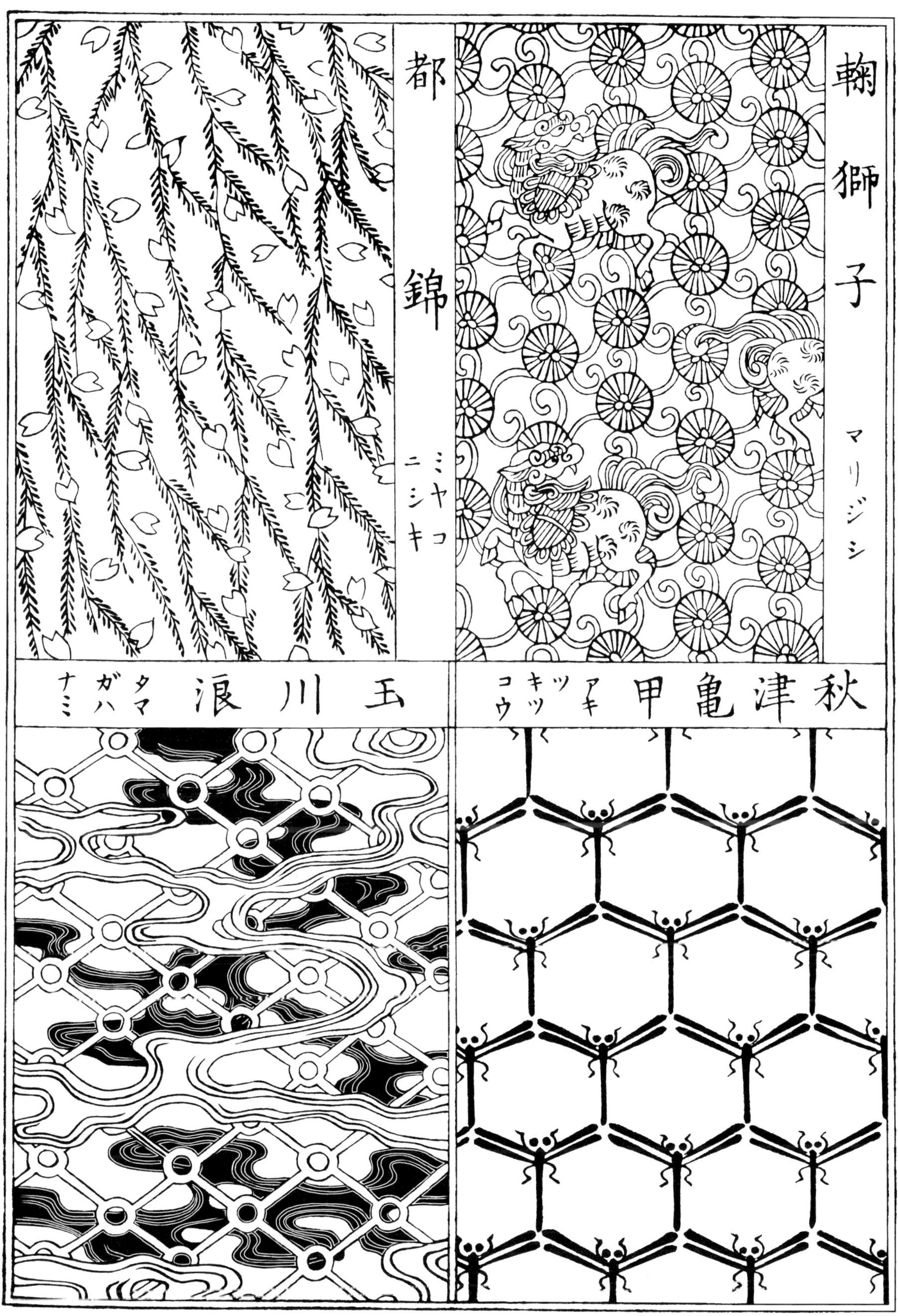
鞠獅子
マリジシ
都錦
ミヤコニシキ
秋津亀甲
アキツキッコウ
玉川浪
タマガハナミ

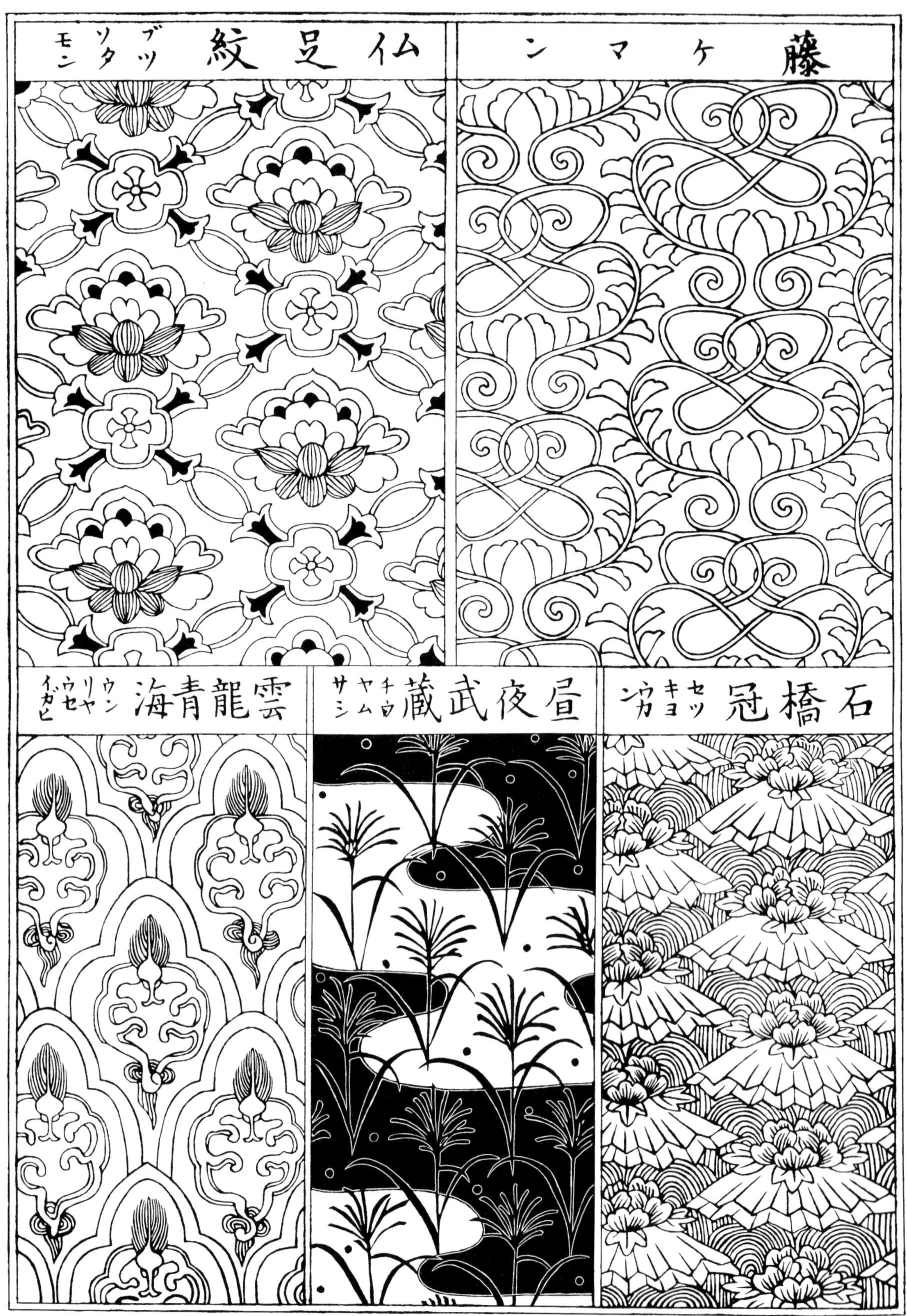
仏足紋 ブツソクモン
藤ケマン
雲龍青海 ウンリヤウセイガイ
昼夜武蔵 チウヤムサシ
石橋冠 セツキヨウカン

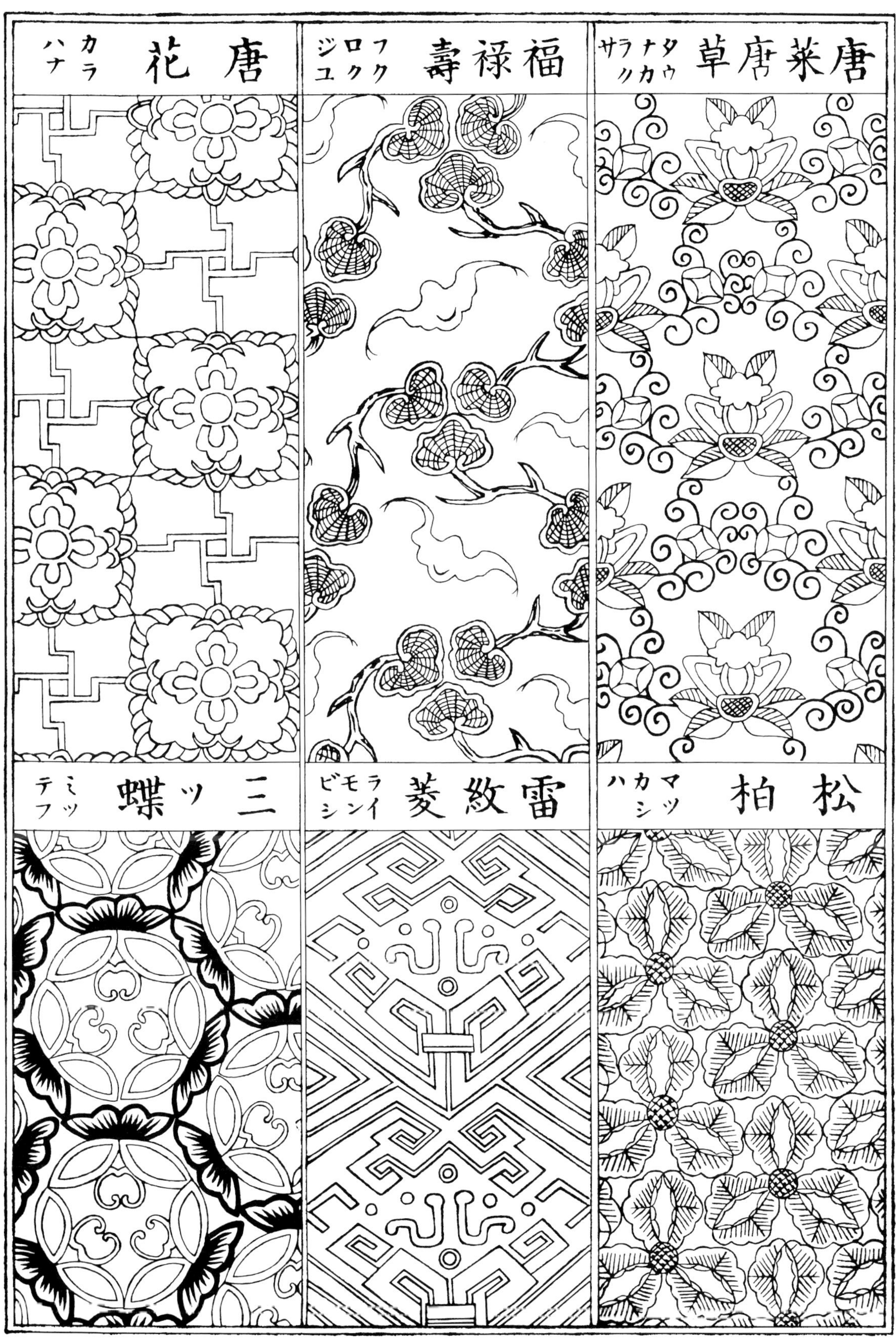
唐花 カラハナ
福禄寿 フクロクジユ
唐莱唐草 タウナカラクサ
三ツ蝶 ミツテフ
雷紋菱 ライモンビシ
松柏 マツカシハ

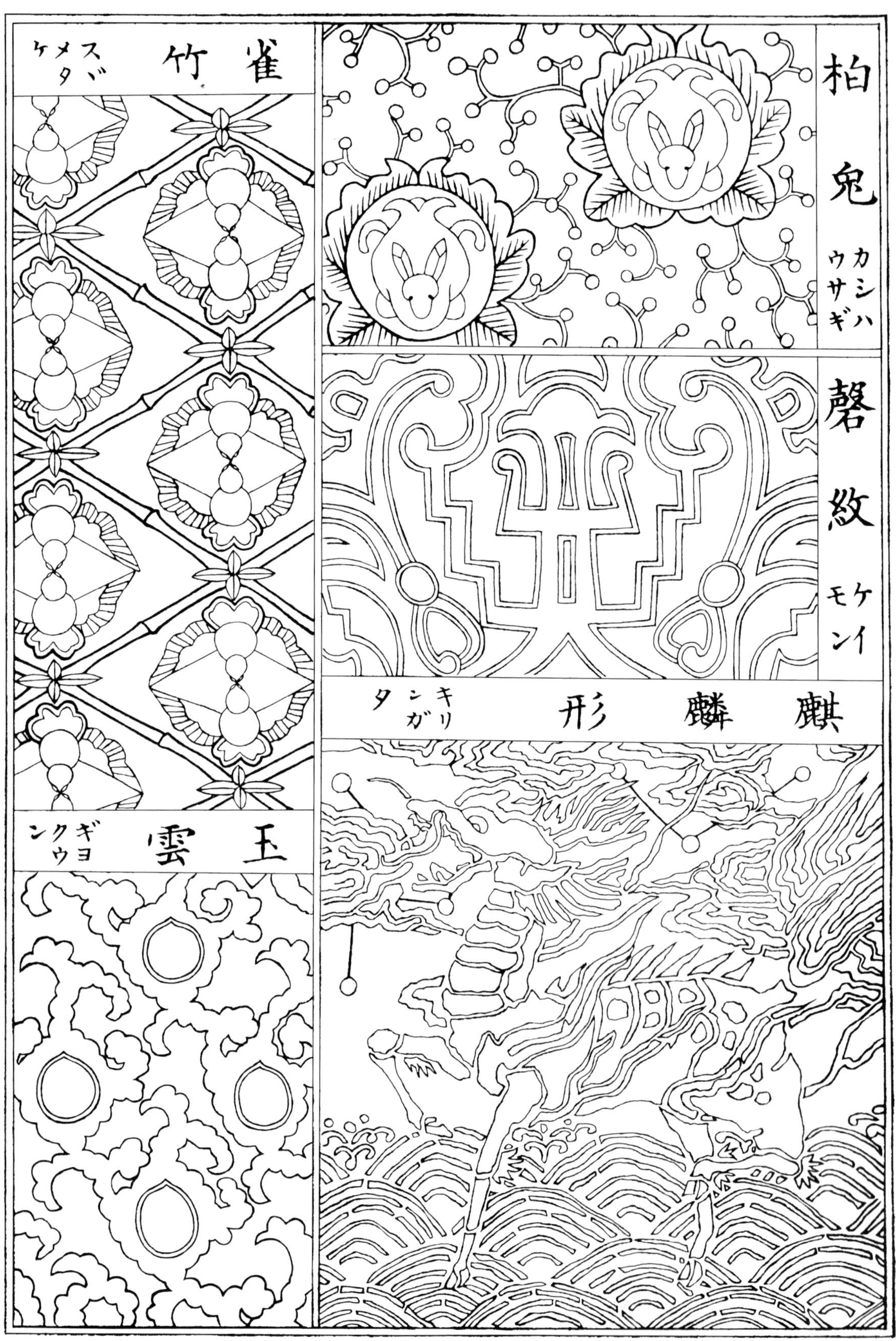

雀竹 スズメタケ
柏兎 カシハウサギ
磬紋 ケイモン
麒麟形 キリンガタ
玉雲 ギヨクウン

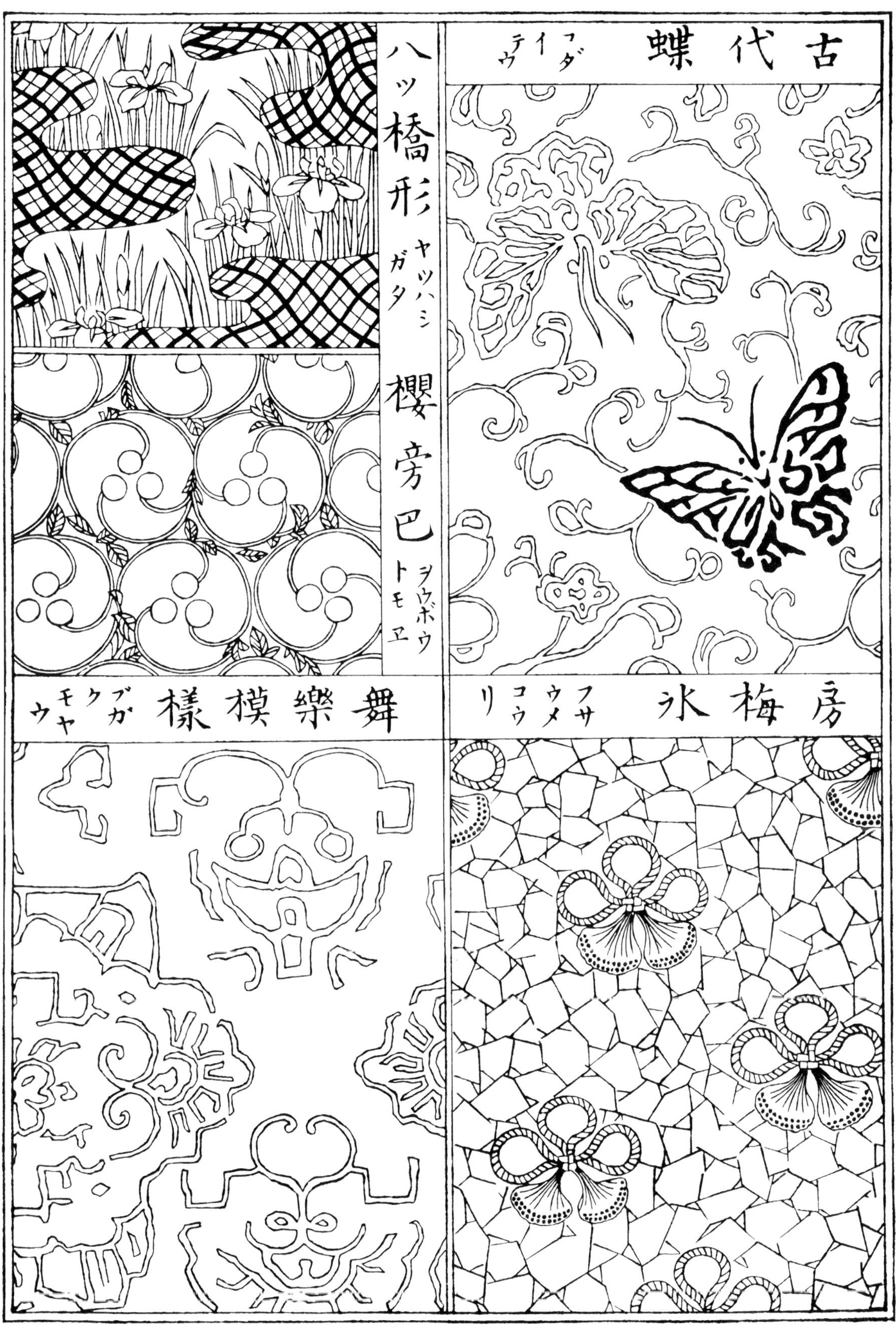
古代蝶
コダイテウ
八ツ橋形
ヤツハシガタ
櫻旁巴
ヨウボウトモヱ
房梅氷
フサウメコウリ
舞樂模様
ブガクモヤウ

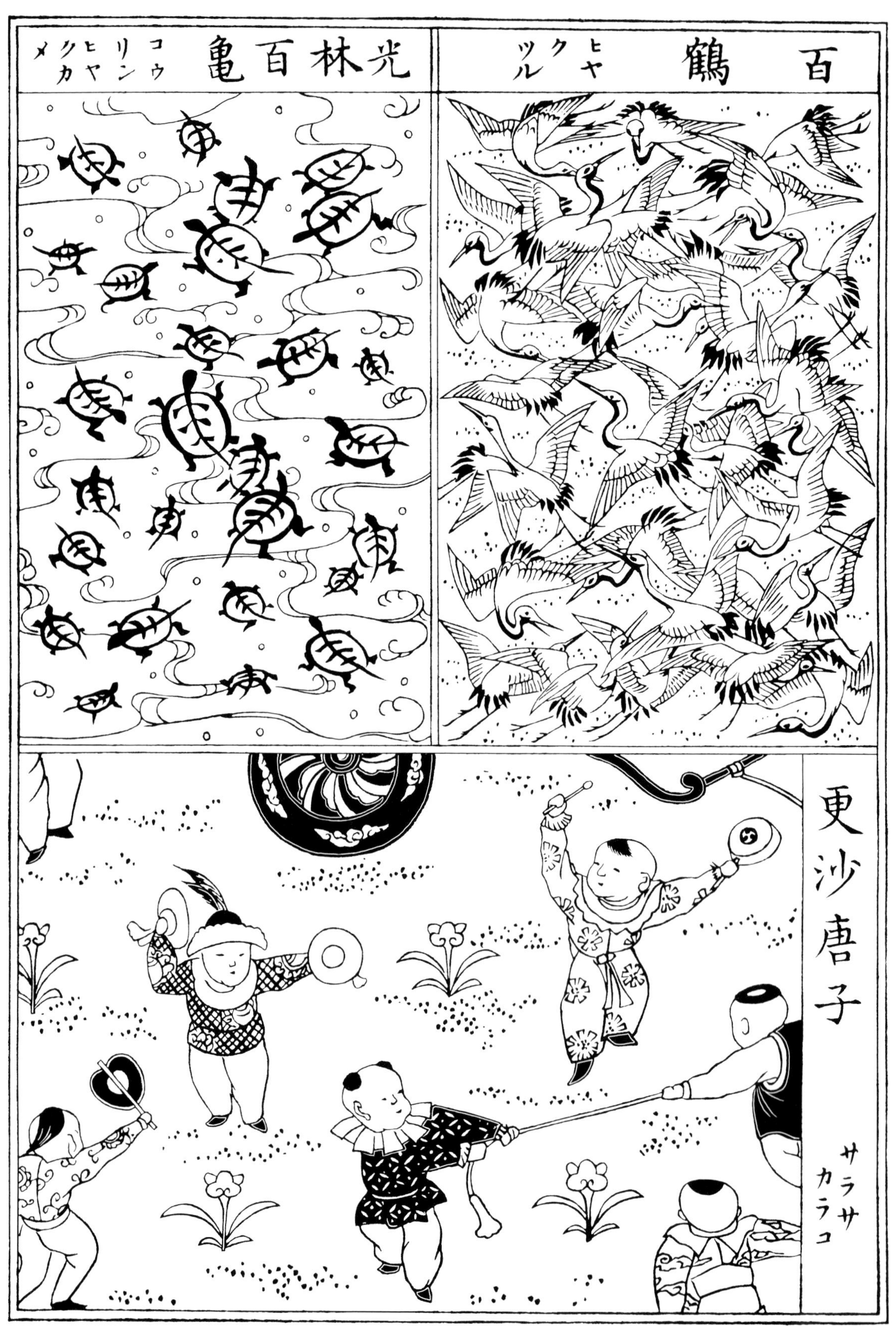

光林百亀
コウリンヒヤクカメ
百鶴
ヒヤクツル
更沙唐子
サラサカラコ

解説
解說
Descriptions

Page 17

FROM LEFT TO RIGHT, TOP TO BOTTOM

Karamon <Lacquerware/wallpaper> Arabesque;
Enshu <Pottery> Design from Enshu (alternative name for the ancient province of Totomi);
Mukairyukodomon <Bronze/cloisonné> Tradional dragon design, used on bronze work;
Marijishi <Pottery> Balls and lions;
Kujakukumo <Pottery> Peacocks and clouds;
Chojugyo <Pottery> Bird, animal and fish;
Kumonamikarakusa <Pottery> Clouds and waves arabesque;
Kiritsuru <Pottery> Paulownias and tendrils;
Totsuruhana <Lacquerware/wallpaper> Chinese design of tendrils and flowers;
Karamon <Bronze/cloisonné> Arabesque;
Wakamatsubishi <Pottery> Young pines and water-chestnuts;
Karamon <Lacquerware/wallpaper> Arabesque;
Mukairenjaku <Lacquerware/wallpaper> Peacock design;
Enshu <Pottery> Design from Enshu (alternative name for the ancient province of Totomi);
Wakukarako <Lacquerware/wallpaper> Border arabesque

Page 18

FROM LEFT TO RIGHT, TOP TO BOTTOM

Horinkiritake <Lacquerware/wallpaper> Phoenixes, kirin (giraffe), paulownias and bamboo;
Kutsuwacho <Pottery> 'Horse-bits and butterflies';
Kawarishichiho <Pottery> Changing cloisonnés;
Tachibanacho <Pottery> Oranges and butterflies;
Hoomaru <Lacquerware/wallpaper> Phoenix design;
Unryo <Embroidery> Clouds and dragons;
Karamon <Pottery> Arabesque;
Zakurokarakusa <Embroidery> Pomegranate arabesque;
Tsurukiri <Lacquerware/wallpaper> Tendrils and paulownias;
Kodomon <Bronze/cloisonné> Traditional design, used on bronze work;
Tsurukarakusa <Bronze/cloisonné> Tendrils arabesque;
Renjakukarahana <Pottery> Peacocks arabesque;
Tsubamefuji <Embroidery> Swallows and wisteria;
Shochikubaishichiho <Lacquerware/wallpaper> Pines, bamboo and plum blossom cloisonné;
Tatsunami <Embroidery> Breaking waves

Page 19

FROM LEFT TO RIGHT, TOP TO BOTTOM

Ryotomoe – Dragon whirls;
Takaranozarashi – Pearls in the open;
Raimon – Thunder pattern;
Karamon – Arabesque;
Kumocho – Clouds and butterflies;
Bussokuren – Buddha's foot and lotuses;
Kawarihagoromo – Feather design;
Biwazuru – Loquats and tendrils;
Sotomon – Elephants head pattern;
Tamahamiryo – Dragons eating jewels;
Fukubemokko – Gourds and cucumbers;
Uchiwakikko – Fans forming a tortoise-shell design;
Hoshiamiseigai – Drying nets and blue sea design;
Inamon – Ears of rice design;
Kumozuru – Clouds and tendrils

Page 20

FROM LEFT TO RIGHT, TOP TO BOTTOM

Hamankyuri <Pottery> Leaves, tendrils and cucumbers;
Kumozuru <Embroidery> Clouds and tendrils;
Karamon <Bronze/cloisonné> Arabesque;
Kikukikko <Pottery> Chrysanthemums forming a tortoise-shell design;
Saitsutakazura <Embroidery> Sai (rhinoceros), ivy and tendrils;
Katawaguruma <Pottery> Wheels and tendrils;
Jujitsunagi <Lacquerware/wallpaper> Crosses;
Kanhoo <Embroidery> Rings and phoenixes;
Yoshirobebishi <Embroidery>;
Karamon <Bronze/cloisonné> Arabesque;
Nanban <Pottery> So-called European design;
Sumanoomokage <Pottery> Suma design;
Omushokko <Bronze/cloisonné> Parrot pattern;
Kumokomori <Embroidery> Clouds and bats;
Tokanotsuru <Embroidery> Potter's tendrils;

Page 21

FROM LEFT TO RIGHT, TOP TO BOTTOM

Togyo <Pottery> Lanterns and fish;
Mukairyuzu <Pottery> Dragon design;
Kakukarakusa <Lacquerware/wallpaper> Arabesque;
Chikuhana <Pottery> Bamboo flowers;
Totetsumon <Pottery> Design used on Chinese iron work;
Hyotsuru <Lacquerware/wallpaper> Gourds and tendrils;

Unchukirin <Pottery> Kirin (giraffe) in the clouds; Fukujutatewaki <Pottery> Fountain of happiness and longevity; Seiajiro <Lacquerware/wallpaper> Gongs and wickerwork pattern; Hanagatsumi <Embroidery> Flowering rushes; Mukaihoo <Embroidery> Phoenix design; Tetsumonryu <Bronze/cloisonné> Dragon design; Uzunami <Pottery> Whirlpool and waves; Karamon <Bronze/cloisonné> Arabesque; Zakurobishi <Pottery> Pomegranates and water-chestnuts

Page 22

FROM LEFT TO RIGHT, TOP TO BOTTOM

Totetsumon <Bronze/cloisonné> Design as used on Chinese iron work; Hojumon <Embroidery> Hojumon design; Takarabishi <Lacquerware/wallpaper> Arabesque; Tsurukame <Embroidery> Cranes and turtles; Totetsumon <Bronze/cloisonné> Design as used on Chinese iron work; Tsurukamemanji <Pottery> Cranes, turtles and swastikas; Karamon <Bronze/cloisonné> Arabesque; Kodomon <Pottery>Traditional design used on bronze work; Karamon <Embroidery> Arabesque; Kodomon <Pottery>Traditional design used on bronze work; Karamon <Pottery> Arabesque; Tsurukikubishi <Embroidery> Tendrils, chrysanthemums and water-chestnuts; Totetsumon <Bronze/cloisonné> Design as used on Chinese iron work; Kodomon <Pottery>Traditional design used on bronze work; Kawarishobugata <Bronze/cloisonné> Water-lily or iris pattern

Page 23

FROM LEFT TO RIGHT, TOP TO BOTTOM

Mancho <Bronze/cloisonné> Ivy leaves; Kanunomon <Bronze/cloisonné>; Amakumoryu <Lacquerware/wallpaper> Rain, clouds and dragons; Yotsushippo <Pottery> Four cloisonnés; Yaetessen <Pottery> Clematis; Inasuzume <Bronze/cloisonné> Sparrows with ears of rice; Marijishi <Pottery> Lions and balls; Okouchi <Pottery>; Mitsuzakuro <Pottery> Pomegranate design; Akitsukikko <Lacquerware/wallpaper> Insects forming a tortoise-shell-design; Kanhanabishi <Lacquerware/wallpaper> Flower design; Azuchigata <Pottery>; Miyakonishiki <Embroidery> Kyoto brocade design; Reishitsuru <Embroidery> Aubergine stalks and tendrils; Yodononami <Lacquerware/wallpaper> Waves in a pool

Page 24

FROM LEFT TO RIGHT, TOP TO BOTTOM

Mitsucho <Pottery> Butterfly design; Karanakarakusa <Pottery> Arabesque; Tamagawanami <Pottery> Waves on the River Tama; Kashiwausagi <Lacquerware/wallpaper>Oaks and rabbits; Matsukashiwa <Lacquerware/wallpaper> Pines and oaks; Fuji <Lacquerware/wallpaper> Wisteria Keimon <Bronze/cloisonné> Gong pattern; Fukurokuju <Pottery> Happiness and longevity; Bussokumon <Pottery> Buddha's feet pattern; Suzumetake <Pottery> Sparrows and bamboo; Raimonbishi <Bronze/cloisonné> Thunder and water-chestnuts pattern; Chuyamusashi <Embroidery> Musashi design; Gyokukumo <Pottery> Jewels and clouds; Karahana <Pottery> Arabesque; Unryuseigai <Pottery> Clouds, dragons and blue sea design

Page 25

FROM LEFT TO RIGHT, TOP TO BOTTOM

Karamon <Pottery> Arabesque; Keimon <Bronze/cloisonné> Gong pattern; Totetsumon <Bronze/cloisonné> esign as used on Chinese iron work; Karahanazuru <Pottery> Chinese flowers and tendrils; Komorikarakusa <Embroidery> Bat arabesque; Keimon <Bronze/cloisonné> Gong pattern; Karamon <Pottery> Arabesque; Karamon <Pottery> Arabesque; Tatsunamibishi <Pottery> Breaking waves and water-chestnuts; Komoribishi <Pottery> Bats and water-chestnuts; Chotsurukarakusa <Bronze/cloisonné> Butterflies and tendrils arabesque;

Uzutsunagi <Lacquerware/wallpaper> Row of whirlpools;
Chozuru <Pottery> Butterflies and tendrils;
Tatsunamimon <Pottery> Breaking waves and gates;
En'unmon <Pottery> Ducks and clouds pattern;

Page 26
FROM LEFT TO RIGHT, TOP TO BOTTOM
Kodaikarakusa <Bronze/cloisonné> Traditional arabesque;
Tsurushokkou <Embroidery> Tendril pattern;
Ryuseikainami <Pottery> Dragons, blue
sea and waves;
Hanagiri <Embroidery> Flowering paulownias;
Totetsumon <Bronze/cloisonné> Design as used on Chinese iron work;
Musubinoshi <Bronze/cloisonné> Knots and bows;
Tamaryo <Bronze/cloisonné> Jewels and dragons;
Sasakikko <Embroidery> Bamboo grass forming a tortoise-shell design;
Karamon <Bronze/cloisonné> Arabesque;
Tsurumon <Embroidery> Tendril pattern;
Karamon <Bronze/cloisonné> Arabesque;
Enshu <Pottery> Design from Enshu (alternative name for the ancient province of Totomi);
Tsurugiri <Bronze/cloisonné> Tendrils and paulownias;
Matsubaguruma <Embroidery> Wheels of pine needles;
Karamon <Pottery> Arabesque

Page 29
TOP Tennin bugaku komoyo – Ancient pattern of angels playing bugaku (court dance music)
BOTTOM Kakukaramon – Rectangular arabesque pattern

Page 30
TOP LEFT Hoomon – Phoenix pattern
TOP RIGHT Hyotsuru – Gourds and tendrils
CENTRE LEFT Tetsumonryo – Dragon design
BOTTOM LEFT Zakurobishi – Pomegranates and water-chestnuts
BOTTOM RIGHT Keiajiro – Gongs and wickerwork pattern

Page 31
TOP LEFT Mukairyonami – Dragons and waves design
CENTRE LEFT Shishibotan – Lion and peonies design
BOTTOM LEFT Totetsumon – Design as used on Chinese iron work
RIGHT Kaichuhoju – Pearls in the sea

Page 32
TOP LEFT Chikuka – Bamboo flowers
TOP RIGHT Fukuju tatewaki – Fountain of happiness and longevity
BOTTOM LEFT Togyo – Lanterns and fish
BOTTOM CENTRE Karamon – Arabesque pattern
BOTTOM RIGHT Mukaihoo – Phoenix design

Page 33
TOP Unchukirin – Kirin (mythological beast, identified with the giraffe) in clouds
CENTRE LEFT Uzunami – Whirlpool waves
CENTRE RIGHT Hanagatsumi – Flowering rushes
BOTTOM Kumouzuryo – Swirling clouds and dragons

Page 34
TOP LEFT Karamon – Arabesque pattern
TOP RIGHT Takarabishi – Arabesque
BOTTOM LEFT Tsurukikubishi – Tendrils, chrysanthemums and water-chestnuts
BOTTOM RIGHT Kametsurumanji – Turtles, cranes and swastikas

Page 35
TOP LEFT Totetsumon – Design as used on Chinese iron work
TOP RIGHT Kawarishobugata – Water-lily or iris design
CENTRE LEFT Kodomon – Traditional design as used on bronze work
BOTTOM LEFT Karamon – Arabesque pattern
BOTTOM RIGHT Hojumon pattern

Page 36
TOP Kodomon – Traditional design as used on bronze work
CENTRE Totetsumon – Design as used on Chinese iron work
BOTTOM LEFT Karamon – Arabesque pattern
BOTTOM RIGHT Tsurukame – Turtles and cranes

Page 37
TOP Kodomon – Traditional design as used on bronze work
SECOND DOWN Totetsumon – Design as used on Chinese iron work
THIRD DOWN Totetsumon – Design as used on Chinese iron work
BOTTOM Keimon – Gong pattern

Page 38
TOP Tsurushishi – Lions and tendrils
CENTRE Tatsunamitsuru – Billowing waves and tendrils
BOTTOM LEFT En'unmon – Ducks and clouds pattern
BOTTOM RIGHT Uzutsunagi – Rows of whirlpools

Page 39
TOP Horyu – Dragon design
SECOND DOWN Keimon – Gong pattern
THIRD DOWN Komorikarakusa – Bats and arabesque
BOTTOM Karamon – Lotus arabesque

Page 40
TOP LEFT Karamon – Arabesque pattern
TOP CENTRE Tatsunamimon – Billowing wave gates
TOP RIGHT Chotsurukarakusa – Butterflies and tendrils arabesque
BOTTOM LEFT Amaryoraimon – Rain, dragons and thunder
BOTTOM RIGHT Hoohanagiri – Phoenixes and flowering paulownias

Page 41
TOP LEFT Komoribishi – Bats and water-chestnuts
SECOND DOWN ON LEFT Amaryo – Rain and dragons
THIRD DOWN ON LEFT Chotsuru – Butterflies and tendrils
BOTTOM LEFT Totetsumon – Design as used on Chinese iron work
TOP RIGHT Karahanazuru – Chinese flowering water-chestnuts
BOTTOM RIGHT Karamon – Arabesque pattern

Page 42
TOP LEFT Musubinoshi – Bows
TOP RIGHT Fukurokuju – Happiness and longevity
BOTTOM LEFT Karamon – Arabesque pattern
BOTTOM RIGHT Ryuseigaiha – Dragons and waves design

Page 43
TOP Enshu – Design from Enshu (alternative name for the ancient province of Totomi)
CENTRE Ban'eryo – Dragon design
BOTTOM LEFT Kamomeryusui – Seagulls and flowing water
BOTTOM CENTRE Tsurushokuko – Tendrils design
BOTTOM RIGHT Karamon – Arabesque pattern

Page 44
TOP LEFT Sasakikko – Bamboo grass forming a tortoise-shell design
TOP CENTRE Rin'uzu – Kirin (mythological beast, identified with the giraffe) and whirlpools
TOP RIGHT Totetsumon – Design as used on Chinese iron work
BOTTOM LEFT Kodaikarakusa – Arabesque
BOTTOM CENTRE Matsubaguruma – Wheels of pine-needles
BOTTOM RIGHT Karamon – Arabesque pattern

Page 45
TOP LEFT Fukurokuju – Happiness and longevity design
TOP CENTRE Hanagiri – Flowering paulownias
TOP RIGHT Fukurokuju – Happiness and longevity
BOTTOM LEFT Tsurumon – Tendril pattern
BOTTOM CENTRE Tamaryo – 'Jewels and dragons' design
BOTTOM RIGHT Wakuhamishishi – Lion pattern

Page 46
TOP LEFT Totsuruhana – Chinese tendrils and flowers
TOP RIGHT Tsurugiri – Tendrils and paulownias
CENTRE Mukairyokodomon – Traditional dragon design as used on bronze work
BOTTOM Chojugyo – Bird, animal and fish

Page 47
TOP LEFT Enshu – Design from Enshu (alternative name for the ancient province of Totomi)
TOP CENTRE Wakukarako – Arabesque
TOP RIGHT Karamon – Arabesque
BOTTOM LEFT Wakamatsubishi – Young pines and water-chestnuts
BOTTOM CENTRE Kiritsuru – Paulownias and tendrils
BOTTOM RIGHT Kujakukumo – Peacocks and clouds

Page 48
TOP LEFT Karamon – Arabesque
TOP RIGHT Kirihotsuru – Paulownias, phoenix and crane
CENTRE LEFT Marijishi – Lions and balls design
CENTRE RIGHT Enshu – Design from Enshu (alternative name for the ancient province of Totomi)
BOTTOM LEFT Kumonamikarakusa – Clouds and waves arabesque
BOTTOM RIGHT Tsurukirin – Tendrils and kirin (mythological beast, identified with the giraffe)

Page 49
TOP LEFT Unryo – Clouds and dragons
TOP RIGHT Karamon – Arabesque
CENTRE LEFT Tsurugiri – Tendrils and paulownias

CENTRE RIGHT Mukairenjaku – Peacock design
BOTTOM LEFT Shoshogiku – Men and chrysanthemums design
BOTTOM RIGHT Kawarishichiho – Changing cloisonné

Page 50
TOP LEFT Hoomaru – Phoenix design
TOP RIGHT Renjakukarahana – Peacocks and Chinese flowers
CENTRE LEFT Zakurokarakusa – Pomegranate arabesque
CENTRE RIGHT Tachinami – Breaking waves
BOTTOM LEFT Tsurukarakusa – Tendrils arabesque
BOTTOM RIGHT Kutsuwacho design

Page 51
TOP LEFT Karamon – Arabesque
TOP RIGHT Shochikubaishichiho – Pine, bamboo and plum blossom cloisonné
CENTRE LEFT Kodomon – Traditional design as used on bronze work
CENTRE RIGHT Horinkiritake – Phoenixes, kirin (giraffes), paulownias and bamboo
BOTTOM LEFT Tsurukamekumonami – Cranes, turtles, clouds and waves
BOTTOM RIGHT Tachibanacho design

Page 52
TOP LEFT Raimon – Thunder pattern
CENTRE LEFT Bussokuren – Buddha's foot and lotuses
TOP RIGHT Tsubamefuji – Swallows and wisteria
BOTTOM Sotomon – Elephant heads pattern

Page 53
TOP LEFT Takaranozarashi – Pearls in the open
TOP CENTRE Kumozuru – Clouds and tendrils
TOP RIGHT Uchiwakikko – Fans forming a tortoise-shell design
BOTTOM LEFT Kumocho – Clouds and butterflies
BOTTOM CENTRE Horin – Phoenixes and kirin (giraffes)
BOTTOM RIGHT Biwazuru – Loquats and tendrils

Page 54
TOP LEFT Ryotomoe – Dragon whirls
TOP RIGHT Fukubemokko – Gourds and cucumbers
CENTRE LEFT Karamon – Arabesque
CENTRE RIGHT Horaikame – Turtle from the Island of Eternal Youth
BOTTOM LEFT Kawarihagoromo – Feather design
BOTTOM RIGHT Inamon – Ears of rice pattern

Page 55
TOP LEFT Hoshiamiseigai – Drying nets and blue sea
TOP RIGHT Tamahamiryo – Dragons eating jewels
BOTTOM Karamon – Arabesque

Page 56
TOP Katawaguruma – Wheels and tendrils
CENTRE LEFT Sumanoomokage – Suma (=Kobe) design
CENTRE RIGHT Yojirobebishi design
BOTTOM Hanabune – Water-flowers and boats

Page 57
TOP Naminichidorijishi – Waves, birds and lion
CENTRE Tokanotsuru – Potter's tendrils
BOTTOM Kumozuru – Clouds, tendrils and cranes

Page 58
TOP LEFT Kanhoo – Phoenix design
TOP RIGHT Saitsutakazura – Sai (mythical animal, identified with the rhinoceros), tendrils and ivy
CENTRE Nanban – So-called European design
BOTTOM Kumokomori – Clouds and bats

Page 59
TOP Hamankiuri – Leafy ivy and cucumbers
CENTRE LEFT Karamon – Arabesque
CENTRE CENTRE Jujitsunagi – Crosses
CENTRE RIGHT Kikukikko – Chrysanthemums forming a tortoise-shell design
BOTTOM Omushokko – Parrot pattern

Page 60
TOP Amakumoryu – Rain, clouds and dragons
CENTRE Inasusume – Sparrows with ears of rice
BOTTOM LEFT Azuchigata
BOTTOM RIGHT Mitsujakuro – Pomegranates

Page 61
TOP LEFT Yaetessen – Clematis
TOP RIGHT Yodononami – Waves in a pool
CENTRE RIGHT Hiryu – Flying dragon
UPPER BOTTOM LEFT Okouchi
LOWER BOTTOM LEFT Kanhanabishi – Flower design
BOTTOM RIGHT Kanunomon

Page 62
TOP Kayomon – Rice leaf pattern
CENTRE Reishizuru – Aubergine stalks and tendrils

BOTTOM LEFT Natsunoiriai – Summer sunset
BOTTOM CENTRE Yotsushippo – Four cloisonnés
BOTTOM RIGHT Man'yo – Ivy leaves

Page 63
TOP LEFT Miyakonishiki – Kyoto brocade design
TOP RIGHT Marijishi – Lions and balls
BOTTOM LEFT Tamagawanami – Waves on the River Tama [or, Jewels, river and waves]
BOTTOM RIGHT Akitsukikko – Insects forming a tortoise-shell design

Page 64
TOP LEFT Bussokumon – Buddha's feet pattern
TOP RIGHT Fuji – Wisteria
BOTTOM LEFT Unryuseigai – Clouds, dragons and blue sea
BOTTOM CENTRE Chuyamusashi – Musashi [name of a province] day and night pattern
BOTTOM RIGHT Sekkyokan design

Page 65
TOP LEFT Karahana – Arabesque
TOP CENTRE Fukurokuju – Happiness and longevity pattern
TOP RIGHT Karanakarakusa – Arabesque
BOTTOM LEFT Mitsucho – Butterflies design
BOTTOM CENTRE Raimonbishi – Thunder pattern and water-chestnuts
BOTTOM RIGHT Matsukashiwa – Pines and oaks

Page 66
TOP LEFT Suzumetake – Sparrows and bamboo
TOP RIGHT Kashiwausagi – Oaks and rabbits
CENTRE RIGHT Keimon – Gong pattern
BOTTOM LEFT – Jewels and clouds design
BOTTOM RIGHT Kiringata – Kirin (giraffe) pattern

Page 67
TOP LEFT Yatsuhashigata – Iris and water pattern
CENTER LEFT Obotomoe – Cherry whirl
TOP RIGHT Kodaicho – Butterfly design
BOTTOM RIGHT Fusaumekori – Tassels, plum blossoms and ice
BOTTOM LEFT Bugakumoyo – 'Court music' pattern

Page 68
TOP LEFT Korinhyakukame – A hundred turtles' design
TOP RIGHT Hyakutsuru – Hundred cranes' design
BOTTOM Sarasakarako – Chinese children playing

Corresponding designs

Page 17
FROM LEFT TO RIGHT, TOP TO BOTTOM
48TL; 47TL; 46TR
48CL; 47BR; 46B
48BL; 47BC; 46TL
49TR; 47BL; 47TR
49CR; 48CR; 47TC

Page 18
FROM LEFT TO RIGHT, TOP TO BOTTOM
51CR; 50BR; 49BR
51BR; 50TL; 49TL
51TR; 50CL; 49CL
51CL; 50BL; 50TR
52TR; 51TR; 50CR

Page 19
FROM LEFT TO RIGHT, TOP TO BOTTOM
54TL; 53TL; 52T
54CL; 53BL; 52CL
54BR; 53BR; 52B
55TR; 54TR; 53TR
55TL; 54BR; 53TC

Page 20
FROM LEFT TO RIGHT, TOP TO BOTTOM
59T; 57T; 55B
59CR; 58TR; 56T
59C; 58TL; 56CR
59CL; 58C; 56CL
59BL; 58B; 57C

Page 21
FROM LEFT TO RIGHT, TOP TO BOTTOM
32BL; 31TL; 29B
32TL; 31BL; 30TR
33T; 32TR; 30BR
33CR; 332BR; 30CL
33CL; 32BC; 30BL

Page 22
FROM LEFT TO RIGHT, TOP TO BOTTOM
36C; 35BR; 34TR
36BR; 32TL; 34BR
36BL; 35CL; 34TL
37T; 35BL; 34BL
37 2nd from TOP; 36T; 35TR

Page 23
FROM LEFT TO RIGHT, TOP TO BOTTOM
62BR; 61BR; 60T
62BC; 61TL; 60C
63TR; 61CL; 60BR
63BR; 61B; 60BL
63TL; 62C; 61TR

Page 24
FROM LEFT TO RIGHT, TOP TO BOTTOM
65BL; 65BR; 63BL
66TR; 65BR; 64TR
66CR; 65TC; 64TL
66TL; 65BC; 64BC
66BL; 65TL; 64BL

Page 25
FROM LEFT TO RIGHT, TOP TO BOTTOM
40TL; 39 2nd from TOP; 37 2nd from TOP
41TR; 39 2nd from BOTTOM; 37B
41BR; 39B; 38C
41TL; 40TR; 38BR
41 3rd from TOP; 40TC; 38BL

Page 26
FROM LEFT TO RIGHT, TOP TO BOTTOM
42TL; 43BC; 42BR
45TC; 44TR; 42TL
45BC; 44TL; 42BL
45BL; 44BR; 43T
46TR; 44BC; 43BR

Other books with free CD Roms by The Pepin Press – Agile Rabbit Editions

90 5768 001 7	1000 Decorated Initials
90 5768 003 3	Graphic Frames
90 5768 004 1	Batik Patterns
90 5768 005 x	Floral Patterns
90 5768 006 8	Chinese Patterns
90 5768 007 6	Images of the Human Body
90 5768 009 2	Indian Textile Prints
90 5768 010 6	Signs & Symbols
90 5768 011 4	Ancient Mexican Designs
90 5768 012 2	Geometric Patterns
90 5768 013 0	Art Nouveau Designs
90 5768 014 9	Menu Designs
90 5768 016 5	Graphic Ornaments
90 5768 017 3	Classical Border Designs
90 5768 018 1	Web Design Index
90 5768 020 3	Japanese Patterns
90 5768 021 1	5000 Animals
90 5768 023 8	Occult Images
90 5768 022 x	Traditional Dutch Tile Designs
90 5768 024 6	Bacteria And Other Micro Organisms
90 5768 025 4	Compendium of Illustrations
90 5768 026 2	Web Design Index 2
90 5768 027 0	Mediæval Patterns
90 5768 028 9	Islamic Designs
90 5768 029 7	Persian Designs
90 5768 030 0	Weaving Patterns
90 5768 032 7	Patterns of the 19th Century
90 5768 033 5	Baroque
90 5768 034 3	Renaissance
90 5768 036 X	Turkish Designs
90 5768 037 8	Lace Motifs
90 5768 038 6	Embroidery
90 5768 039 4	How to Fold
90 5768 040 8	Folding Patterns for Display and Publicity
90 5768 041 6	Russian Designs
90 5768 043 2	Rococo
90 5768 044 0	Structural Package Designs
90 5768 045 9	Web Design Index 3
90 5768 046 7	Erotic Images
90 5768 047 5	Fruit
90 5768 048 3	Vegetables
90 5768 049 1	Mandalas
90 5768 050 5	The Agile Rabbit Book of Pictures
90 5768 051 3	The Agile Rabbit Book of Historical and Curious Maps
90 5768 052 1	Astrology

More titles in preparation

In addition to the Agile Rabbit series of book+CD-ROM sets, The Pepin Press publishes a wide range of books on art, design, architecture, applied art and popular culture. Please visit www.pepinpress.com for more information.